WITHDRAWN

for Hannah

. . . 'our deepest fear is not that we are inadequate.

Our deepest fear is that we are powerful beyond measure.

It is our light, not our darkness, that most frightens us.'

We ask ourselves, Who am I to be brilliant, gorgeous, talented and fabulous?

Actually, who are you *not* to be?

You are a child of God.

Your playing small doesn't serve the world.

There is nothing enlightened about shrinking so that other people won't feel insecure

around you.

We are all meant to shine, as children do.

We were born to make manifest the glory of God that is within us.

It's not just in some of us; it's in everyone.

And as we let our own light shine,

we unconsciously give other people permission to do the same.

As we're liberated from our own fear, our presence automatically liberates others.

Marianne Williamson, *A Return to Love*

girlosophy

A SOUL SURVIVAL KIT

anthea paul

photography by Chris L. Jones

ALLEN&UNWIN

First published in 2000

Allen & Unwin
83 Alexander Street
Crows Nest NSW 2065
Australia
Phone: (61 2) 8425 0100
Fax: (61 2) 9906 2218
Email: info@allenandunwin.com
Web: www.allenandunwin.com

National Library of Australia
Cataloguing-in-Publication entry:

Paul, Anthea.
        Girlosophy: a soul survival kit.

        ISBN 1 86508 432 8.

        1. Young women – Conduct of life. 2. Spiritual formation.
        3. Young women – Life skills guides. 4. Self-realization.
        5. Self-perception in women. 6. Women and spiritualism.
        I. Jones, Chris (Christopher Lloyd), 1957– . II. Title.

305.23550994

Art direction and styling by Anthea Paul
Design by Barnum Group Design, Sydney, Australia
Photography by Chris L. Jones Photography, Sydney, Australia
Illustrations by Cathy Derksema, Masterpeace, Sydney, Australia
Edited by Jude McGee, Sydney, Australia
Girlosophy CD produced by Tom Middleton, London, UK
Legal counsel: John Martin, Allen Allen & Hemsley, Sydney, Australia;
Julie Robb, Banki Haddock Fiora, Sydney, Australia

'Exodus' written by Bob Marley. Lyric reprint courtesy or the Marley Estate.
Publishers – Bob Marley Music/Rykomusic Ltd/Festival Music Pty Ltd.

Printed in China by Everbest Printing Co. Ltd

10 9 8 7 6

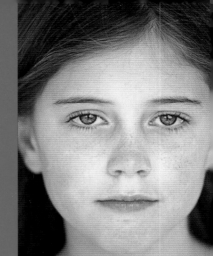

contents

Introduction

I wrote this book to pass on a few of my hard-learned lessons to those young women and girls in search of clues about how to navigate this increasingly pressured and competitive world. So if you're a seeker and you want some answers, this book is for you!

The thoughts contained herein hopefully provide an alternative to the self-help books that many of us turn to when the going gets rough. The trouble with many so-called self-help books, I have found, is that by the time you come to discover them, you're usually old enough and experienced enough not to need them; or they are obsolete by the time you finally find them; or they are too specific without broad application.

I felt that the commonsense advice that we are given in dribs and drabs, or that we often learn through expensive mistakes, could be given as early as possible and in consolidated form. A lot of the ideas and information in *girlosophy – a soul survival kit* are things I wish I had known, understood and taken to heart much earlier in my life. Such is the nature of the Universe, however, without whose timely lessons I never would have grown in the ways that I have, and which has led me to write this in the first place, in order to fulfill at least a part of my destiny.

Reflecting the truth that each one of us perceives uniquely, I felt the visual element that is mostly lacking in traditional self-help books would be the key to taking *girlosophy* to another level, and would allow readers to interpret for themselves what was personally relevant. I wanted my book to be both a joy to look at *and* an inspiration to read. Hopefully *girlosophy* is the sort of book that can be picked up each day, opened at any page and be both creatively inspiring and uplifting.

Girls often write to magazine advice columns hoping to resolve issues in their lives. Many of those issues that pop up again and again are problems that are centuries old. But there are new ones too, specific to our time, which, it seems, many young women are struggling with. And the times are changing so quickly that our mothers, even if they are in the cut and thrust of the modern world, may not be aware of the kinds of new issues facing their daughters. It would also appear that the self-esteem of many of these young women has been undermined, even at a time when they have, in theory, unprecedented freedom and opportunity. *girlosophy* aims to provide a starting point for girls to deal with these new issues, and to increase their self-confidence. Hopefully readers will feel better about themselves as a result.

While I have included a few things that may be classed as 'etiquette', I am not focusing on 'behavioral rules' as such. These are things that I hope readers will do naturally as a result of thinking in a new way and their greater awareness. The idea is to enable those who read the book to design their own code of ethics and behavior, rather than operate within some imposed rigid structure. I have always believed people should do what they really feel in their heart is right for them, as long as they avoid hurting others in the process. As the saying goes, the mind, once expanded by a thought, never returns to its original shape. This book can never replace good parenting, but I hope it can be a complementary tool to assist in bridging gaps and in helping young women take charge of their lives.

The photographs in the book are all taken of *real* girls – they are not professional models – aged between three and thirty-two, from all over the world. They were chosen mainly for their energy and personality as opposed to the traditional mainstream criteria for modeling, which are based purely upon physical characteristics or 'beauty'. Beauty is still the most narrowly subjective concept, the bandwidth for which needs urgent expansion, and while the 'girlosophy girls' are each uniquely beautiful, they are more importantly beautiful in spirit.

Above all, I believe that as early as possible women need to develop a personal code of behavior and ethics by which to live. It is critical to develop individual and personal rules and boundaries – to determine those things that are acceptable and those that are unacceptable. Once these are in place, hopefully we can come to understand that abiding by what are now our own rules – or not abiding by them – has much bearing on the subsequent patterns of events in our lives. We can go with our hearts and take great leaps of faith into the unknown on a more sustained basis if we know a solid platform is in place. I would like to add here that I, too, am still learning, and there's plenty for me to grasp and reflect upon, even as I peruse my own writings.

In the future I look forward to seeing all young women rise up to fulfill their individual potential, as is their birthright. As the great French writer and girlosopher Simone de Beauvoir once said, 'One is not born a woman, one becomes one.'

A portion of the proceeds of this book will go towards establishing a foundation to help young women of all nationalities have the chance to express themselves and find their true essence. I dedicate this book to the eternal girl in all of us. My deepest thanks to those who have inspired and helped me on my journey, and I wish you every success on yours . . .

Anthea Paul, 21st century

girlosophy: it's your life – think about it!

You will need:

- an open heart and an open mind
- an understanding of the spirit within
- a desire to overcome all obstacles in achieving your individual destiny
- an understanding of the need for persistence
- a tenaciousness that is unique but not dogged
- the will to continue learning
- a direct and honest approach
- a search for personal challenges and self-improvement
- an aspiration for spiritual growth
- an acceptance of change and loss
- the courage to fail
- the courage to try again
- calculated risk-taking behavior
- a strong vulnerability
- the ability to ask for things clearly
- the ability to say no firmly
- an ornate simplicity
- a refusal to be made to feel insecure by anyone
- a propensity to focus and build on positive life experiences
- the relentless pursuit of excellence
- a ruthless compassion
- a dedication to finding the truth in every situation
- acceptance of fear and aggression as valid sources of personal power
- the resolve to walk away when necessary.

CONSTRUCTION ZONE!
WARNING:
WORKS IN PROGRESS
REAL GIRLS AHEAD
WEAR YOUR HARD HAT!

girl:

[def:n] A young person; a female child; a young woman; source of the feminine spirit.

growing   inspired

[chakra: crown chakra; the individual connecting with the Universe]

radiant   light

girl

Hannah is wearing amethyst and tourmaline crystal talismans

INNOCENT WISDOM.
A TRUE ILLUSION.FRESH.
SPIRITED.SWEET.
NOT SO SWEET.
ENERGIZED.HOPEFUL.
NAUGHTY.GOOD.LIGHT.FREE.
A CANVAS FOR LIFE.
READY.OR NOT.
SINGLE-MINDED.
CONFUSED.PLAYFUL.
SULKY.NEEDY.MOODY.
CONNECTED.
LOST IN A MOMENT.
SECRETIVE.OPEN.
WILLING.LEADING.
FURTIVE.AFFECTIONATE.
HAPPY.SPONTANEOUS.
UNCONTROLLED.
CONTROLLING.SAD.
NURTURING.CARING.
EXCITED.AUTHENTIC.
MATERIAL.RUTHLESS.
DARING.CHANGEABLE.
LA NIÑA.THE GIRL CHILD.
EVER PRESENT.THE FUTURE.

life: [def:n] The state of being alive, the living form, containing and generating energy; the essential or inspiring idea (of a movement etc.); animation; spirit; one who or that which imparts spirit or animation; the active side of existence; a state of spiritual regeneration as opposed to a worldly or material state of mind; the thing to treasure and be excited about; a situation, object or being possessing constant flowing energy or life force.

love

infinite

[chakra: root chakra; the individual being linked with the physical world]

f e

free-flowing   energy

GIRL SCOUTS

life throws curve balls. be prepared! expect the unexpected!

RULE!

appreciation

preparation

consideration

cultivation

thankfulness

the art of living

Appreciate the smallest thing, whether a smile, a card,
a fragrance in passing, a lovely view, a creature

Take care with the rituals of your life – the preparation of food,
making your bed, bathing, dressing, phone calls to your friends
or family

Consider carefully the effects on other people of all of your actions,
words and thoughts
Everything eventually comes back – multiplied

Cultivate an understanding of other cultures and viewpoints even
when – especially when – it's difficult to put yourself in their place

Be thankful for every meal, every glass of fresh water,
every comfort in your home

Be gracious in both victory and defeat

Be courteous and gentle in your habits

Love and cherish your friends and family

Respect your planet and yourself

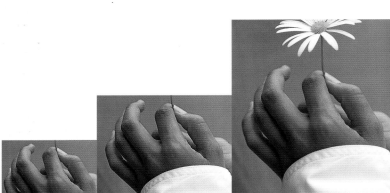

the art of living

Isis, Australia

get your signals straight – what message are you sending? Your clothes, your voice, your mannerisms, movements and attitudes: they all reveal *you* to the world. Be conscious of your own subtext. And when *you* want to know what's really going on, **look and listen.**

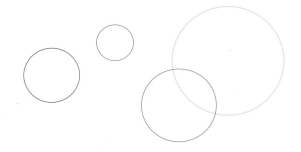

sending
signals
straight

what's in or out

is not caring

what's in . . . .

get rid of the clutter!

Your immediate environment reflects your life. Clutter, dirt or mess around you shows things are out of control.

Keep your personal space well ventilated, ordered, clean and clutter-free. Make it a sanctuary for total wellbeing.

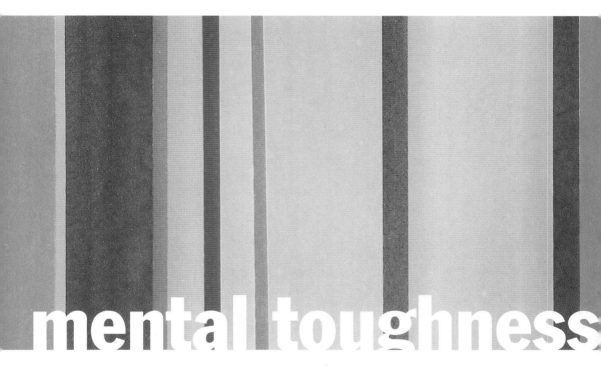

mental toughness

To survive and to succeed, you need to be tough – mentally tough!

Not everyone is born with **MENTAL TOUGHNESS**, but anyone can cultivate it through personal discipline and **COMMITMENT.** Living through and overcoming difficult times nurtures mental toughness.

It means you can talk yourself into going to the gym when you least feel like it. It means you can still get out of bed when you'd rather pull the covers up and hide from the world.

Mental toughness helps you **STAY THE DISTANCE** to the winners' circle.

I t's the hardest game of all, because the rules aren't given to you to begin with. The first difficulty is that you are already playing before you even realize it! Then comes the discovery that not only are you 'IN' but you don't necessarily have all of the rules by which to play.

The Game of Life

In the Game of Life there are three types of rules: outside laws – laws that the community agrees upon and abides by; the natural laws – laws that instinctively feel right to you; and the Universal laws – the 'umbrella' rules that are the highest spiritual laws. We all operate within these three categories of rules and we're meant to discover, learn and amalgamate parts of all three. There's no 'pretending' either: once you are conscious of the rules, you can't go back to being ignorant of them.

Once you have a deep-seated understanding of these laws and how certain things affect and are affected by your actions and thoughts, you will develop your own personal set of rules that you can apply to the infinite variety of situations that life serves up. As you live, you will gather lessons from which you can construct a personal code that is constantly changing and growing.

By developing your own code you have made a sort of pact with your soul and accordingly your karma. Break your own law, pay your own penalty (remember, pain is nature's warning!). But the beauty of this is that life itself can teach you the rules, so if you pay attention and try to learn from all of your mistakes as you go, through reflection and contemplation, pretty soon you'll only be repeating the positive things that resulted in progress.

It may take several repetitions of a pattern for you to understand that you are either not recognizing or you are deliberately breaking a personal law, which is why on occasions you may feel as though you're being hammered by life. But this is part of the process of development.

It's a bit like Snakes and Ladders – you climb the ladder only to fall down the snake on the next roll of the dice. It can be a freaky trip sometimes, but life's like that, and sometimes you just gotta roll the dice and go with it.

Say NO and *mean* it

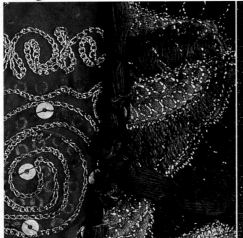

If someone asks you to do something you don't want to, it's easy — say no! You don't need an excuse: a polite SMILE and a firm 'No' is enough. Don't give in. When people refuse to hear your MESSAGE, it's all the more reason to say NO and move on.

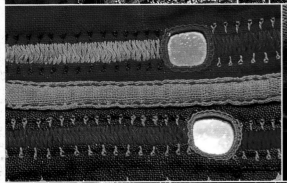

If you want to be sure you've got the gig
If someone's promising you the world
If they *say* they're on the same page you are
And you want to see what the real deal is
If you'll believe it when you see it, then
Get it in WRITING!

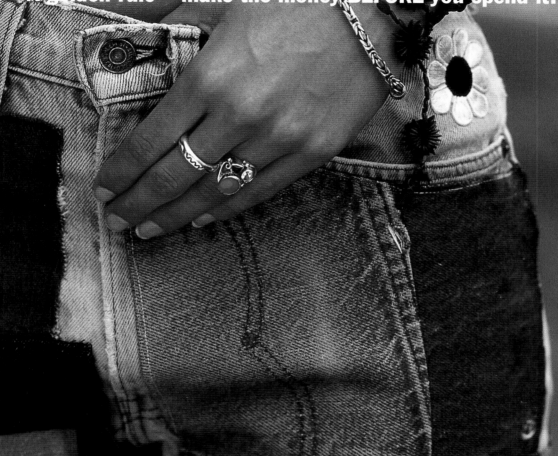

Budgeting is like weight control – if you don't keep an eye on the figures, they start to add up . . . Budgeting is *way* cool.
A golden rule – make the money BEFORE you spend it!

The minute you receive payment for work you have done for someone else:
1. Pay the Universe (charity work, tithing, service)
2. Pay yourself and your future (saving, investing)
3. Pay back the Earth (bill payments, gifts, recycling, awareness).

karma

What you did yesterday will bear fruit in what you do and who you are today.

This is karma in action. Karma is a Sanskrit term, and is also known as the law of

cause and effect. It's a doctrine which states that everything you do – good or

bad – has a consequence. You can influence destiny by exercising your free will in a

certain way. The beauty of this is that karma can be built up and it can also be

'burned off'. Every new day is a chance to change your destiny.

karma.destiny.
good.bad.action.
consequence.
cause.effect.
bea   will.
de   ge.
life.p   .soul.
pre   ure
kar   iny.
good   tion.
co   ce.
ca   ct
beauty.freewill.
deed.change.
life.past.pact.soul
present.future

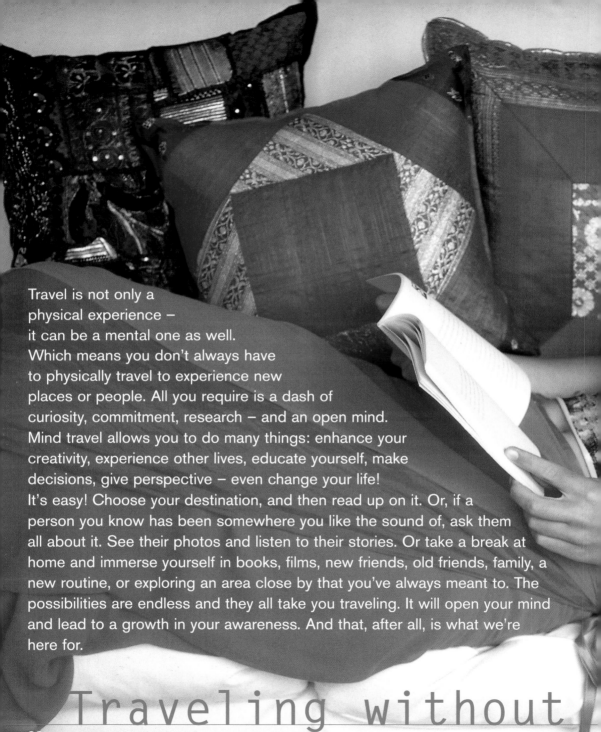

Travel is not only a
physical experience –
it can be a mental one as well.
Which means you don't always have
to physically travel to experience new
places or people. All you require is a dash of
curiosity, commitment, research – and an open mind.
Mind travel allows you to do many things: enhance your
creativity, experience other lives, educate yourself, make
decisions, give perspective – even change your life!
It's easy! Choose your destination, and then read up on it. Or, if a
person you know has been somewhere you like the sound of, ask them
all about it. See their photos and listen to their stories. Or take a break at
home and immerse yourself in books, films, new friends, old friends, family, a
new routine, or exploring an area close by that you've always meant to. The
possibilities are endless and they all take you traveling. It will open your mind
and lead to a growth in your awareness. And that, after all, is what we're
here for.

Traveling without

moving

SAY

NO

TO

DRUGS

BE
MiND-FULL
NOT MiND-LESS

Your body is a divine gift.

It is both your property and your responsibility.

Protect it, treat it well.

No one can touch, claim or use it, unless you allow it.

You decide who is allowed into your personal space.

Let no one transgress it by physical or other means.

Be assertive and vigilant to ensure you are not being compromised in any way.

Be aggressive if someone is trying to take advantage of you.

Do whatever is in your power.

Sometimes strength is as much a state of mind as it is a physical quality —

and you may be capable of more than you think.

your body is a divine gift

CHILDREN: SHOULD YOU / SHOULDN'T YOU?

Children should be planned for. ✿ Don't just go on autopilot. Think it through first. ✿ Having children may be one of the most creative and important things you ever do, but you need to plan for them and be prepared for all the changes they will make to your life. Children are an enormous responsibility and there are many things to consider. ✿ Are there people around you to support you when you need it? They might be friends, family or a clinic nurse or counselor. ✿ Can you financially afford to keep and raise a child? ✿ If you don't have a partner, or your partner was no longer around, could you do it on your own? ✿

Whatever you decide, children should ideally be planned for...

How is your health? Are you well and energetic enough to keep up with children? Are you prepared to devote yourself and your time to someone who is almost totally dependent on you for their safety and wellbeing? ✿ How will you deal with the changes that children will bring to your relationship, your career, your life? ✿ You can choose not to have children. That's okay, too. What matters is that you think about it, and that *you* make the choice. ✿ YOU DECIDE.

**IT'S A SERIOUS STEP.
DON'T JUST GO ON AUTOPILOT.
THINK ABOUT IT.**

BRAVE NEW GIRL

You need **BUTTERFLIES** in your **HEART** – not in your stomach!

The good thing about decisions is that most of them can be changed simply by making another. So, if it looks (or feels) like it was the wrong decision and things aren't quite panning out the way you'd like, don't let it become a mental prison: **MAKE ANOTHER DECISION.** It's that easy. Besides, you can't sit on the fence forever, and all it takes to make a change is a leap of faith. Whatever the eventual outcome, at least it's bound to be interesting!

HAVE **FAITH** AND REMEMBER
it takes
COURAGE.

Often in life you might take a wrong turn, but at the time you may not be aware that it *is* a wrong turn. So you'll coast along for a while, thinking that the scenery looks a bit different to what you expected, but that things seem okay. It may take ages, but suddenly you might come up against an immoveable boulder on the path, one you can't climb over or go around. Or the road you are on ends at a cliff with the equivalent of the Grand Canyon beyond. This is the moment of truth, when you realize not only that you took a wrong turn, but that you're going to have to retrace your steps. You may feel so very far from your destination that you despair, and you *just can't believe* that you wasted your time, how stupid of you, etc. etc.

The path to self-determination is steep and deep

DON'T DESPAIR! Don't give yourself a hard time, either. If you think back and look really hard there will have been something positive (maybe many things) that came out of your little detour. It doesn't matter that you made a side journey: it was just that – a side journey – and it won't necessarily prevent you from reaching your true destination. It just means that you weren't concentrating, or you need to be more 'on it' if you really want to get where you're going.

Time passes and so does the moment. Soon you'll be back on the right path. Reality checks in at different times with different hats on. The view from the top is always changing and rarely, if ever, replicates itself. Getting anything that's worthwhile is always full of wrong turns, dead ends and sometimes dark despair. But that serves to make it all the sweeter when you finally arrive.

say never!

never mistake kindness for weakness

never take advantage of another person's time or good will

never stoop to conquer

never think you'll get away with it

never forget where you came from

never give up

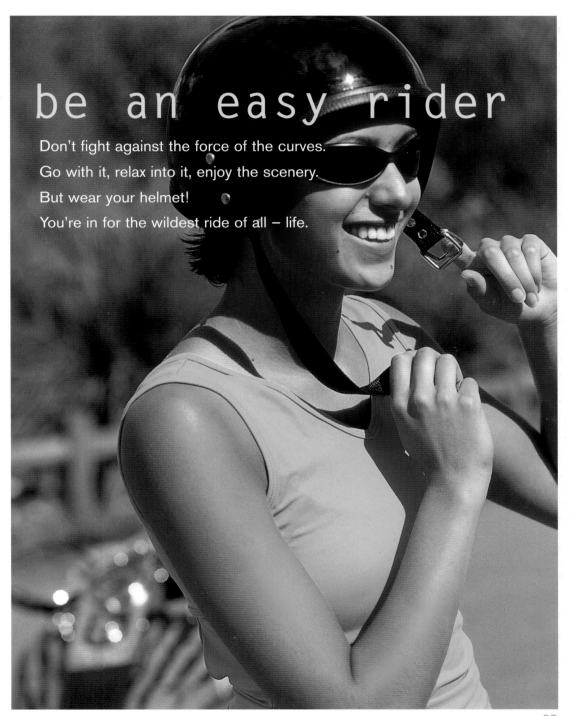

be an easy rider

Don't fight against the force of the curves.

Go with it, relax into it, enjoy the scenery.

But wear your helmet!

You're in for the wildest ride of all – life.

A

sk questions of everyone about everything, including yourself. The more questions you ask, the more you stimulate your mind and the more creativity you will reap from it in turn.

reflect

reveal

refer

revi

works.

release

rejoice

ew

renew

seize every moment

Consciously 'seize' every moment, because an idea only takes seconds and a few seconds can change your personal universe entirely.

life is
for **doing**
and enjoying

life is for doing and enjoying, not for having and acquiring, owning or gaining.

we are borrowing everything on the physical plane, even our bodies.

the way to really live your life is to realize this truth and get on with enjoying

the amazing things in the physical world, whatever your position is within it.

the most beautiful things in the world are not owned by anyone.

purpose: [def:n] The end or aim, object or intention, design; meaning, effect, result, consequence, to have an intention or be bound for a place or destination.

purp

persistent   understanding   responses   purely

[chakra: root chakra; the foundation for self-expression and ambition, tempered by the desire to evolve, protect and survive]

objective   sincerely   expressed

FOCUS on

Focus on your goal
with laser precision
and an unbending will.

Do not be deterred by all
of the distractions that
the Universe will throw at you like a test.

And each distraction *is* a test,
just to see
how committed you really are.

your **GOAL**

YOU CAN'T GET LOST

ON A STRAIGHT ROAD

How do you find your true calling?

How do you find what it is you are meant to do with your life?

1. Know yourself well: understand the package that you are, the weaknesses, strengths, likes, dislikes, talents, faults.
2. Get some good advice: what's out there?
3. Experiment, experiment, experiment: keep on trying different things until you find what really feels right for you.
4. Develop a thicker skin so you can turn rejection into experience.
5. Find a mentor or role model.
6. Do what you love to do. If you can't, make what you're doing a strategy to get you doing what you *want* to do.
7. Have a realistic game plan and stick to it, no matter who or what says you can't.
8. Prioritize.
9. Be yourself.

You make your own luck.

Find yourself.

You will have to be creative.
Seek different outlets for expression.
Set yourself a challenge. Develop your own expectations of yourself
and measure yourself against yourself.
Ignore other people's agendas and stick to yours.
The person you find will be the one *you* created.

You.

Stand up straight
Don't cross your legs
Take a cardigan
Stand up straight
Don't cross your legs
Take a cardigan
Stand up straight
Don't cross your legs
Take a cardigan
Stand up straight
Don't cross your legs

Sometimes your mother really does know best

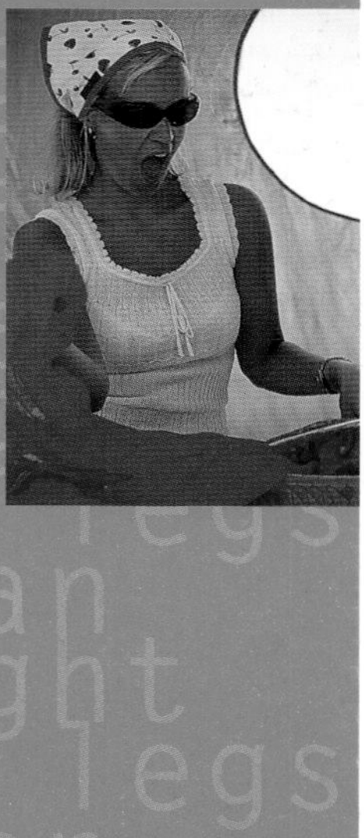

Take a cardigan
Stand up straight
Don't cross your
Take a cardigan
Stand up straight
Don't cross your
Take a cardigan
Stand up straight
Don't cross your legs
Take a cardigan
Stand up straight
Don't cross your legs

49

ARE YOU **MATCH FIT**? YOU NEED TO HAVE MORE THAN JUST A BELIEF IN SOMETHING TO TRULY ACCOMPLISH A GOAL. YOU NEED **STAMINA** TO OVERCOME AND MEET ALL OF THE OBSTRUCTIONS AND BARRIERS THAT WILL PRESENT THEMSELVES ALONG THE WAY. YOU NEED **STRENGTH** TO ENABLE YOU TO PRESS ON WHEN THE GOING IS RUGGED. YOU NEED **REST** AND **RECOVERY** SO YOU CAN BACK UP AND DO WHATEVER IS NECESSARY, OVER AND OVER AGAIN. AS LEGENDARY FOOTBALL COACH VINCE LOMBARDI ONCE SAID, 'KEEP YOURSELF IN **PEAK** PHYSICAL CONDITION BECAUSE FATIGUE MAKES COWARDS OF US ALL.'

51

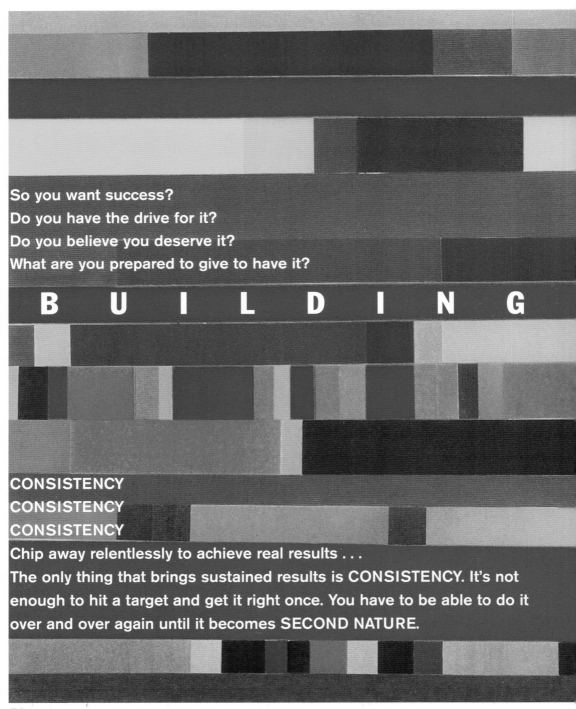

So you want success?

Do you have the drive for it?

Do you believe you deserve it?

What are you prepared to give to have it?

BUILDING

CONSISTENCY

CONSISTENCY

CONSISTENCY

Chip away relentlessly to achieve real results . . .

The only thing that brings sustained results is CONSISTENCY. It's not enough to hit a target and get it right once. You have to be able to do it over and over again until it becomes SECOND NATURE.

TO DELEGATE = DECREASED STRESS

TO BE ORGANIZED = INCREASED POWER

B L O C K S

Busy doing . . . NOTHING?

You need to set aside time to reflect. Reflection will reveal your purpose.

Your purpose is your calling in life. Once you've thought it through then

you can get on track and make it happen.

Failure is not an option – because it doesn't exist.

Failure is just one critical step on the path to success.

You can start over any time you choose, no matter what mistakes you made in the past.

You can change anything with a new attitude and a new mindset.

Winners know that it's the comeback that counts.

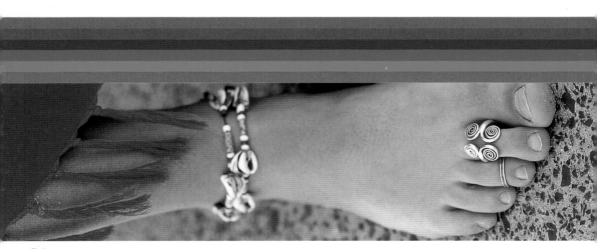

Slipper, Rajasthan, India

control v success

do you want to be in control or

do you want to be successful?

team players win

feed it . . .
raw materials are the first step.

expose it . . .
find a format you like and
show the world.

explore it . . .
variety-it's all good!

train it . . .
get professional backup.

nurture it . . .
keep trying new avenues.

CREATIVITY IS . . . A

express it . . .
don't hold back and
don't give up.

experiment with it . . .
what turns you on?

paint
draw
sing
write
design
sew
knit
craft
build
act
cook
download
sculpt

WORK IN PROGRESS

film
photograph
style
video
produce

feed it . . .

LEARN
TO
FLY
Your mind
was born
with wings
to soar
above reality.

Don't waste them:
use them
to take flight
in your imagination . . .

RUNNING
WITH
THE PACK?
If you want to
achieve stunningly
different results
you need to adopt a
SPECTACULARLY
DIFFERENT
APPROACH.
Running against the pack
will give you the leading edge.
Find out what will work
for you and design and
FOLLOW
YOUR
OWN
PATH.
But remember:
to be yourself
you need to
know yourself first.

STAYING

its no

GROUNDED

mean feat

S ometimes the Universe takes a long time to deliver and you'll need dedication, perseverance and patience to hang in there until it does. But if you want something badly enough, all the Universal laws will conspire to give it to you. It's a matter of when, not if.

hang in there!

Regrets?

The rule is: work hard, play fair and leave no regrets on the field!

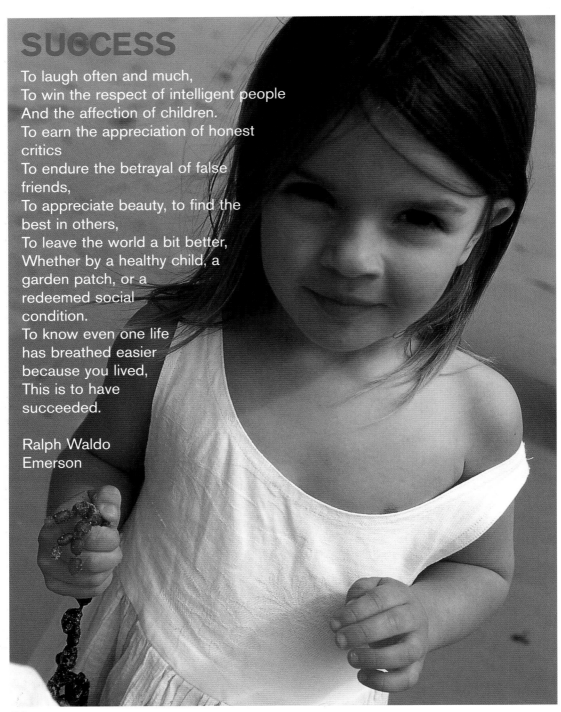

SUCCESS

To laugh often and much,
To win the respect of intelligent people
And the affection of children.
To earn the appreciation of honest
critics
To endure the betrayal of false
friends,
To appreciate beauty, to find the
best in others,
To leave the world a bit better,
Whether by a healthy child, a
garden patch, or a
redeemed social
condition.
To know even one life
has breathed easier
because you lived,
This is to have
succeeded.

Ralph Waldo
Emerson

SUCCESS – what's *your* definition?

We each need a personal definition of what success means to us, one that is uniquely ours and reflects our highly individual goals and paths. Decide on yours as soon as you can, so you can establish what *you* want, not what your parents, your friends or society want *for* you. Success can be anything. It need not be wealth or fame. It need not be material at all. Success can be GIVING to or CARING for others. It can be CREATING something new. But what's most important is that success is what *you* make it. So redefine success as PERSONAL POWER – the power to do what *you* want, ON YOUR TERMS.

INTEREST = INSPIRATION = ACTION

ACHIEVEMENT

YOUR FUTURE LIES IN
YOUR OWN HANDS

love:

[def:n] A feeling of deep regard, fondness, and devotion for; deep affection usually accompanied by yearning or desire for; affection between persons more or less founded on or combined with desire or passion; an unconditional state of bliss and ecstasy with life.

1 0

life   overflows

[chakra: heart chakra; the center point of the chakra system, healing and emotions are generated and balanced by free-flowing love]

v

e

vessel

eternal

It's about TRUST.

When it comes to falling in love

NO chase

NO obsession

NO trying too hard

Just let it be

Real Love

There is no need to rush into a relationship or be in a panic to find a life partner. The time will come when you are ready and the Universe will present someone.

When you least expect it, love will come to you.

So while you are biding your time, prepare the vessel. Find a creative outlet to express yourself and develop a sense of who you are and who you might become. Find yourself *before* you fall in love, so you bring with you everything you need to weather all conditions and the peaks and troughs that are the process of loving.

For love to endure it must be nurtured, especially through the tough times, for these are the times that separate true loves from the wannabes. After all, it is the rarest flower that blossoms in adversity.

To achieve real intimacy in a relationship you need to reveal yourself, to be honest and truthful, to communicate openly. You must surrender your ego, have your flaws scrutinized and accept and love the flaws in another. If you can both be truly intimate in these ways, your love will continue to grow.

The C word

Commitment is emotional intent backed up by action.

Do not ask for a commitment, especially from your partner, because then you will never know if it is real and true.

Commitment isn't something you pledge, it's something you *do.* When they are there beside you, doing all the right things at the right time and in the right way, their commitment will be obvious to you.

Self-love

**Self-love —
the most important kind.**

**There is love in service.
Making others happy is a rare ability and
a gift to be treasured.**

How deep is your love?
Make it your daily offering to the universe.

Shrine offerings, India

LOVE ALL SHARE ALL WHAT GOES AROUND COMES AROUND

Relationships are about give and give, *not* give and take.

give and give

You know you are with the right person when they give as much as you.

not give and take

BE THE BEST FRIEND

W e each need one or two close friends who are constant in our lives. They are people to whom we are instinctively drawn when problems seem insurmountable or when we've lost faith in ourselves or in humanity. They are the ones who can offer a measured, objective response.

To be the best friend to someone that we can be is a commitment. It requires loyalty and a generosity of spirit as unshakeable as it is untradeable, and which never stoops to pettiness or meanness. A best friend forgives foibles, overlooks shortcomings and accepts, even cherishes, idiosyncrasies.

YOU CAN BE

Changes are welcomed and applauded when appropriate, sympathy is automatic and sincere, crises are attended to without judgment, and the willingness to help is in proportion to the ability to do so.

We don't have room in our lives to be best friends to everyone, so it comes down to a chosen few who, once so chosen, are there for the long haul.

Friendships like these are committed relationships and are a reflection of ourselves. As such they are deserving of the utmost respect, for they are a part of us. These friendships are sacred.

What you do with it is up to you. Choose carefully whom you share it with.

Use condoms. Smart girls play it safe always. No ifs, no buts, no excuses. You're protecting your future, not to mention your life.

Love it.

sexuality

Protect it.

Respect it.

— sensuality

Nurture it.

sensuality sensuality sexuality

use it
consciously

Use it wisely.

Men are not the enemy,
even if you've been told they're from Mars.
They can be your best friends.
But if you want to date younger men,
be careful and remember –
big girls shouldn't play with little boys.

Living together or marriage? The big issue

Many couples tire of running across town with toothbrushes and spare underwear in their bags. So they start to talk of moving in together, also known as 'your place or mine?' Others think they might have found 'the one', but want to experience their beloved's habits first hand, *before* they tie the knot. So they decide to live together first.

On the surface, living together is like a trial marriage. But while moving in sounds very mature and sensible, rarely do couples have a long-term goal in mind when they decide to do it.

If you are considering living together, find out what the real deal is. Are you both aiming for long-term commitment and marriage, or is moving in just a convenient solution to a short-term problem?

Ask yourself and your partner what you expect from the new arrangement and whether it fits in with what you ultimately both want in your lives. Think about the big picture. *Hard.* Which brings us to the options:

1. You move in together on the understanding that while you love each other you are really only committed to the situation (the relationship *and* the living arrangement) as long as you both feel like being there. You are not considering marriage – it may not happen at all, and you feel comfortable with that. There are a lot of other people out in the world that you would potentially like the chance to experience, but this works for you, *for the moment.* At this stage and in the foreseeable future you do not want children together. Financially, you plan to split expenses and keep a record of any big-ticket purchases so you can part reasonably easily in the future.

2. You move in together on the understanding that you really want to be together for the rest of your lives and you are both committed to the situation (the relationship *and* the living arrangement) for the long term. You are not considering marriage because neither of you believe in it and you have no pressing reason (religious, cultural or other) to get married. You are both prepared or want to have children together, regardless of whether you're married or not. You are prepared to be as emotionally and financially committed as if you were actually married. You are prepared to make other types of commitment as a couple (for example, buying property, relocating), thus becoming financially involved in each other's lives. You both accept and are happy with this arrangement.

3. You move in together on the understanding that you will treat this phase as a trial marriage. You will agree on how long before you both reassess the situation (the relationship *and* the living arrangement) to decide whether or not it is working and whether you are both sufficiently committed to get married. You agree to live separately again if the answer to any of these questions is either doubtful or negative, or you may decide to give it some further time. You're not inflexible, just realistic. You both believe in marriage and have decided that this is the kind of security in a relationship that you both would like and/or need, prior to becoming more involved financially and emotionally and/or prior to having children. Until this discussion occurs you will split expenses. You both accept and are happy with this type of arrangement.

4. You want to get married and you are only prepared to live with someone, bonding with them emotionally, physically and financially, on the condition that you do marry. Nothing else is an option for you. If this is what you ultimately want, and after a period of several years of living separately, marriage still seems nowhere on the horizon, then you are (a) prepared to let go a relationship that doesn't move to this level of commitment rather than compromise your principles by moving in together; (b) very happy to continue in the relationship for a time limit that you have given yourself; or (c) prepared to go your separate ways in order that you can each have your needs met.

They may sound a bit cut and dried, but those are the options. I'll leave it to you to fill in the flowery bits. Anything else (such as living together because it's cheaper or easier or in the hope that your partner will finally commit) and you're kidding yourself. And if you kid yourself, rest assured you'll be thumped hard by the Universe, because you are meant to respect yourself more than that.

It's not unromantic to make plans – it's smart.
So discuss the issue and prepare yourself for the future.

Marjorie, France

ULTIMATUMS — NOT FOR THE FAINT-HEARTED! NEVER USE AN ULTIMATUM TO BLUFF ANOTHER PERSON. THAT'S MANIPULATION. IF YOU DO ISSUE AN ULTIMATUM TO SOMEONE, BE PREPARED FOR THE POSSIBILITY THAT IT MAY NOT WORK IN YOUR FAVOR. IT'S A HIGH-RISK STRATEGY, AND YOU'LL HAVE TO BE READY TO FACE THE CONSEQUENCES. YOU MAY END UP BEING SATISFIED WITH THE RESULT — OR YOU MAY BE DEVASTATED. EITHER WAY, YOU'LL HAVE TO LIVE WITH THE OUTCOME.

Sunset, Thar Desert, India

HEARTBREAK IS A PART OF LIFE.

Almost everyone has experienced it at least once and we each react differently to the breakdown of a relationship. You can help yourself get through it, though, if you take it on in a proactive way: **REALIZE** that whatever is happening (or not happening) is part of the grand plan the Universe has divined for your highest good. **DECIDE** that you will go through the grief, anger, disbelief and sadness, but ultimately you will recover, to be wiser and having grown. **KNOW** that love is infinite and you can generate as much as you consume. **BELIEVE** there are no limits to love, and in the future you will love another person and be loved more than you can possibly imagine. **REMEMBER** not to be so caught up with crying over a lost skateboard that you miss the Rolls Royce that's parking right in front of you.

Love is addictive. Getting over a break-up hurts like hell.

Going cold turkey is the fastest remedy. Move forward as soon as possible and don't waste time or hinder your progress. Once you're 'clean' you'll have a totally different perspective, not only about the other person but also (and more importantly) about yourself. Here's a 12-step plan to help you get over the addiction:

1. Box up all the photos, letters, mementos and objects that remind you of that person. Be strong – you need to detox. Give them to a friend or family member to store until you are in a new relationship or a new phase in your life.

2. Detox your body. Drink as much water as you can take.

3. Get rid of anything you bought with your ex that you would otherwise have to look at: paintings, rugs, jewelery – whatever.

4. Don't drink alcohol (it's a depressant) or do other drugs.

5. Sell whatever you can and replace it. Objects like your bed can store energy, so it may be best, where possible, to let the key items go. It's a way of ensuring you're not holding on to the past and that the new person in your life won't be tainted by the energy from the old relationship.

6. Eat well. Don't let yourself go. Now is the time to look and feel your best. There's so much to do and the best is yet to come.

7. Move from the place where you lived or did things as a couple. Go somewhere totally new. View it as a chance to start over.

8. If you can't move, renovate, paint or do space-clearing feng shui.

9. Exercise – as much as possible. Get lots of fresh air.

10. Make some new friends to whom you'll be able to talk about your ex without them being torn by loyalty. You'll be able to dish the dirt and let off some steam then move on and rebuild your self-esteem.

11. Go on a trip, either on your own or with a close friend or family member. Generate some new memories and you'll stop taking trips into the past.

12. Meditate. Spend time alone. Think. Plan. Recover.

Change is the only constant

When one person changes in a relationship, the relationship itself changes. Give it time. Develop a new perspective. Realize that this is going to happen many times over if each of you is to reach your full potential as individuals. Accepting and adapting to change is an essential part of being and staying together. Change begets change.

Temple door, Nepal

Never forget that you are a queen . . .

Carefully inspect those who come to court your affections – from the safety of your throne! Stake out your territory and wait for them to declare themselves. Above all, be sure they're not the jester in disguise – or worse!

keep your heart sweet

beauty: [def:n] The quality which gives the eye and other senses intense pleasure; or that characteristic in a material object or an abstraction which gratifies the intellect or the moral feeling; embellishment; grace; charm; adornment.

bea

being   ethereal   ageless

[chakra: heart chakra; aesthetic qualities are filtered into emotions, creating recognition of the eternal in all that is physical]

uty.

uniquely   totally   yourself

godd

ess

you are divine

realbeauty

IS NOT

We are all fascinated by beauty and many of us devote much of our lives to its pursuit. But physical beauty can only ever be held fleetingly. Real beauty is far greater – it's a life force, an energy, which radiates from within and transcends the physical. It's a vibe – you feel it in those who truly know they have it.

Real beauty is not beauty generated purely for others' consumption. Real beauty is beauty in action, not beauty that sits on the sidelines of life, worried it will run or get messed up.

Real beauty may not always be visible at first glance, but it lasts *forever.*

a spectator sport

whatever happened to natural?

REAL
NATURAL
BEAUTY
NEVER
GOES
OUT
OF
FASHION

whatever happened to natural?

The natural woman at the beginning of the twenty-first century is on the brink of extinction. Daily we are bombarded with images of women pumped up, trained, reduced, bleached, waxed, sculpted, covered up, uncovered, perfected, remodeled, recolored. Make a pact with yourself. Dare to be different and construct your own definition of beauty. Don't buy into 'the look'. Real, natural beauty never goes out of fashion.

Protect your

Physical beauty is a poor standard by which to judge anyone.

self-image
DON'T BELIEVE THE HYPE!

WAKE UP –
WHY MAKEUP?

If you're like most girls, you probably have a secret in your bathroom or your handbag – your makeup collection. No doubt you've been adding to it over the years with impulse buys, first-date splurges and special offers, all in the name of beauty.

Most women love to buy makeup. Why? Do we really believe that makeup makes us more beautiful? It's as if we're all competing in the X-Treme Beauty Games. The pity is, there is no winner – except, of course, the cosmetic companies.

In fact makeup and beauty have little in common. Unlike the beauty that makeup creates, real, inner beauty is no illusion – it is reflected in your eyes and it never fades. You can't get it from a product, no matter what promises are made. So, rather than make up your face, make up your mind – to radiate real beauty from *within*.

The more confident you are, the less makeup you'll need, and you can't buy self-esteem in a compact. So never let anything that you see in magazines or advertisements make you feel less about yourself. Learn to discriminate between images that are positive and those that are designed to lower your self-esteem. Don't compare yourself to others – YOU ARE ENOUGH!

And next time you're tooling around at the beauty counter, have another think: what are you really buying – and why?

rather than make up your face, why don't you
MAKE UP YOUR MIND

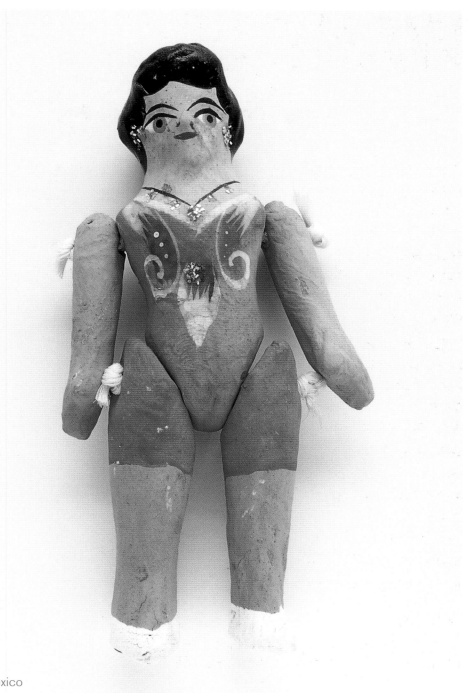

Irma doll, Mexico

KNOW YOUR OWN BEAUTY.
LOVE AND ACCEPT YOURSELF. Feel the **JOY** that is your natural birthright.
EXULT in your own existence, for it is a **MIRACLE** that you are here at all.
Understand that you are connected to all that you admire in the physical
world and that it is merely a manifestation and reflection of all that is beautiful
WITHIN YOU.

DON'T BE A CLONE.

Don't follow anyone or anything slavishly.
SET YOUR OWN TRENDS. Develop your
own style. What do *you* like? What suits *you*?
Don't just follow fashion: take the elements
that work for you. Be true to what suits you
and uniquely represents who you are in
the world.

GOOD SHOES, A GOOD HAIRCUT AND A GOOD ATTITUDE.

MAKE UP YOUR OWN.

If you're not sure, ask people you admire, who have a strongly developed sense of self and a unique style, what they think of your look. Ask them what suits you. After all, it's not brain surgery, it's just clothing. Dressing yourself is a form of self-expression, another chance to be creative. So enjoy the process and remember – you are a work in progress.

work with what you have

mirror mirror . . .

Mirror, mirror on the wall
who's the fairest one of all?
You are, of course.

Your mirror is one of the most potentially powerful – and destructive –
things that you use. You may look in the mirror many times each day, so it's
important to understand the damage you can do to yourself, psychologically
and spiritually, every time you look at your reflection and criticize something.

So instead of being a slave to the mirror, make your mirror work for *you*! In the
morning, don't stand in front of it bemoaning what you don't have or what you
don't like. Apart from the fact that you are showing yourself disrespect,
thoughts and words are very powerful and can manifest the very things you
are focusing on. Instead, concentrate on feeling approval for yourself in every
respect. Find all of your good points and practice smiling and being happy
about them. Will yourself to overlook a pimple or
wrinkle and tell yourself that you are a beautiful
person. Love it all.

Bronze buddha, Indonesia

Start the day positively this way. Not only will you
feel better, you will feel motivated to get out there
and make it happen.

Because *you* deserve it.

Develop a hobby that allows you to create beauty.

Charm

Charm is a quaint and rather old-fashioned word, and these days it is rare

to hear someone described as being 'charming' or of having 'charm'.

People with charm are genuinely interested in others.

They are kind and generous of spirit, unassuming

and delightful to be around. Real charm cannot

be turned on as needed, for it is then revealed to

be a veil for a hidden agenda.

Some of us are born with charm, while others may

need to cultivate it. But we can all have it. It is the result of

focusing on our advantages, so we radiate our best qualities. This in turn

brings out only the best in those around us.

Now that's charming.

DON'T EAT JUNK FOOD.

DON'T THINK JUNK THOUGHTS.

Tighten up your lifestyle – the checklist

While it is essential that you work towards having your emotional and spiritual house in order, you also need to take care of yourself physically. If your lifestyle isn't healthy, you won't be at your best and it will be that much harder to achieve your goals.

The trick to being and looking your best is simple: love life, love yourself and practice a few basic disciplines:

1. Drink lots of water – at least 1.5 liters daily. Water keeps everything fresh and gives you energy. This is the best tip for feeling and looking your best.

2. Eat well and don't diet – dieting creates a mentality of lack. There is no such thing as 'going on a diet' because you are already on one. In fact, you probably need a lot more food than you think, so eat three nutritionally balanced and healthy meals per day. Let your body tell you what it needs to give it energy. And don't eat or drink junk food – if you can't pronounce the ingredients on the label, stay away. Also, try not to skip meals – it plays havoc with your blood sugar levels, your emotions and your metabolism. And remember – fruit and vegetables rule.

3. Take a multivitamin supplement, especially if you are under stress, working harder than usual, traveling, or your usual routine is disturbed or changing.

4. Exercise regularly – start early and stick to it. Join the gym and use it at least three times per week, or find a sport that you can do. Walk. Run. Stretch. Move. Exercise reduces stress, which profoundly affects how you look. Exercise in fresh air as much as possible for maximum oxygen benefits.

5. Protect and look after your skin – face and body – every day. Use sunscreen and moisturizers.

6. Don't smoke – smoking affects your skin, as well as causing all kinds of other health problems.

7. Rest and recover with regular sleep. Work out how much you need in order to perform at your best. Nothing robs you of vitality and health faster than lack of sleep.

8. Avoid or limit alcohol and caffeine – they dehydrate your skin and can cause other health problems. They can also affect your personality if you indulge too much or too often. Alcohol and caffeine should be an occasional treat, not a regular part of your lifestyle. And, of course, any other form of drug taking is a definite no-no. If you want to keep your lifestyle and your mind intact, stay well clear.

9. Observe cleanliness and hygiene – you need to be clean on all levels: mentally, physically and spiritually. Get into having lots of showers and baths and washing your hands frequently to cut down on germs and reduce the transmission of illnesses like colds and flu. Enjoy the sensual side of being clean: pamper yourself in your private time in the bathroom. Clean and floss your teeth at least twice a day: keep them sparkling, so you'll want to smile at the whole world.

10. Look after your hair – have a haircut every six weeks or so. Natural is usually best: only color your hair if you can afford to really maintain it. Don't go for a color that's too radically different from your natural state: nothing looks worse than the roots-growing-out look. And eat well: your hair will love you for it!

11. Care for your hands – they are on display constantly. Keep them in good condition and don't wear too much jewelry or bright polish. Understated is better. The same goes for feet, so check them out – you might get a shock!

12. Relax – meditate daily, have regular massages and practice yoga. Stress reduction is one of the greatest things you can do for your health and your looks.

grace = your natural state

ALL THE RIGHT MOVES

walk, talk and carry yourself gracefully.

hold your head high. look sharp.

meet life head on, but be flexible

enough to bend around it as necessary.

be conscious of your self,

but don't be self-conscious.

NOW YOU'RE *REALLY* MOVING IN THE RIGHT DIRECTION

Ita, Indonesia

Seeing the beauty in everything and everyone is the key to seeing the beauty in yourself. Rising above life's injustices and still holding your head up is the most beautiful thing of all. Focus on the beauty all around you and very soon you will only be able to see yourself that way too. It is within us all and achievable every day we are here on earth.

you are beauty-full (it's true)

healing: [def:n] To make whole, to restore to health; to cure (of disease etc.); to reconcile; regenerate; to set free from guilt; to purify; to grow or become sound or whole.

heal

heart   eventually   adjusts   love

[chakra: lower abdomen chakra; center for balancing the emotions, relationships and creativity]

is   no   game

Lose the excess, for she who travels

lightest travels furthest.

What's your emotional baggage?

Where do you come from?
What do you stand for?
Your roots matter.

They can make you – or break you. Make peace with them, whatever they are, and be proud of your heritage, because it's unique.

Nothing, not even the most difficult upbringing or so-called disadvantaged background, need be a barrier to all the best things in life – friendship, love and happiness.

So don't reinvent or cover up your past. Your story is as interesting as anyone else's. Embrace your own beginnings and you'll find you can embrace the beginnings of others. Whatever culture or tradition you come from, it is part of your history and lineage. It is part of you!

Love everything in your past. Your future depends on it.

roots    past    tradition

peace    story    history

proud    love    embrace

heritage    culture    life

unique    begin    lineage

DETOX YOUR BODY
AND EXPERIENCE A NEW REALITY
PURIFY YOUR SYSTEMS
HAVE **CLEAR** SKIN AND **BRIGHT** EYES
SLOW THE AGEING PROCESS **NATURALLY**
GET OFF THE **MOOD** SWINGS
PREVENT ILLNESS AND DIS-EASE
BECOME MORE CREATIVE
UP YOUR **ENERGY** LEVELS
BE MORE **PRODUCTIVE**
NEED LESS SLEEP
BE MORE **AWARE**
BE LESS TIRED
HEIGHTEN YOUR **SENSES**

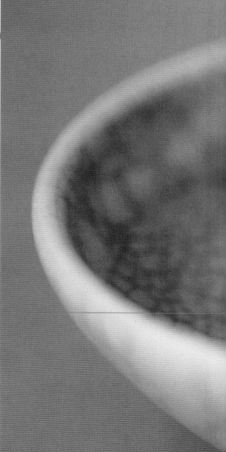

FEEL BETTER — ALL THE TIME!

UNFINISHED BUSINESS

Get closure. Heal all of the rifts in your life.
Apologize if it's overdue. Release anything or
anyone that's hanging over your head.
Speak to someone who's not speaking to
you or to whom you're not speaking.
Forgive them. Forgive yourself. Any
unresolved issues, fallings out or
grudges can hinder
progress and render
you incapable
of flying high
through
life.

FORGIVENESS = HEALING

DON'T GET BITTER – GET BETTER!

not waving, drowning?

Depression is an illness.

Sometimes it's temporary but sometimes it isn't.

Learn to monitor yourself, and look for the signs in both yourself and others. Listen to what you're saying and thinking: is there too much negativity? Can't sleep? No energy? Can't stop crying? Can't get out of your rut? Feeling run-down all the time? Edgy? Lost your appetite? Too much appetite? Or do you just feel like you're not coping? These can all be signals that you are suffering from depression.

DEPRESSION IS AN ILLNESS

Get some help. Talk to someone. Don't let anyone tell you you're being silly or self-indulgent.

And listen to others when they say they're feeling low. If someone says they're going to harm themselves or another person, take it seriously. Tell someone else.

If someone is threatening suicide they may need professional help.

And you may save a precious life.

143

Let it flow, let it flow — there's

nothing wrong with tears.

On the death
of a person close to you,
the end of a love affair or the end
of a situation,
tears are appropriate
in whatever quantities they come.
Tears help cleanse the soul
so the attachment washes away.
Then you can start to let go,
to move forward and
continue with your life.

Save your own life

1. DANGER – Identify the source of imminent or actual danger, anything negative that could harm you or that could be a threat to your equilibrium in a physical or mental sense.

2. RESPONSE – Protect yourself by moving to a position of neutrality (the safety zone) as quickly and calmly as possible. This gives you time to think and react appropriately. Survey the scene for further potential fallout and apply damage control where necessary. Enlist help if you think you're out of your depth.

3. AIRWAY – Clear the airway with specific, open and honest communication, being true to your instincts and what you really feel at all times.

4. BREATHING – Deep, rhythmic, steady. Breathe when you think things are moving too fast. Give yourself breathing space, until you can get a grip. Count ten deep breaths and then as many more as you need until you feel ready to tackle the situation. Breathe to relieve tension or when you need to slow things down.

5. CIRCULATION – Put a stop to any bleeding of your resources. Stop leaching energy. Preserve it. It's your lifeblood. Firm pressure at the source works best. Keep the energy flowing; don't become stagnant. Change up! Exercise your right to the new. Only by closing one door will other doors open for you.

6. DEPTH OF CONSCIOUSNESS – Check in to reality. Examine your own state of awareness. Be consciously and acutely aware of all of your thoughts, actions and observations. Practice and master meditation, and train your mind to behave. Establish clarity through vision and focus on the task ahead.

7. EXAMINATION OF THE BODY AND THE WALLET – The body: Is your body fit for the task of living? Be the best and the most you can be by maintaining your health, as an ongoing commitment to yourself. Exercise can work wonders, and the benefits can include an improved self-image. Simply honoring a commitment to yourself can help your self-esteem. The wallet: How's the stash of cash? You'll need plenty of this stuff for the long road ahead to recovery, so plan and budget for the trip by starting your savings plan early. Don't spend it, save it!

8. ASSESSMENT – Find someone you admire and ask them for feedback to help you get on the right path. You can only grow through experience and by regularly reviewing your progress. Best to find out sooner rather than later if you're off course.

9. SPLINT FRACTURES – Heal all rifts, splint the broken bits, get ready. Build better relationships, even if it means reframing your expectations. Respect that others have a right to feel however they feel. You can't control it, so mend wherever you can. Then, at the very least, you can move forward from a neutral position. And keep on moving – onwards and upwards!

Tree of Life ceramic, Mexico

147

Mindy, United Kingdom

Laugh long. Live longer.

Service with a smile?

When you're down on yourself and things aren't running smoothly, take

time out – change your focus – to help someone else. Surprise them and

maybe you'll surprise yourself. If you help someone at a time when they

need it and when they least expect it,

the law of karma manifests 'the fruit of the deed'. This reflects the

universal truth that someone else will be there in turn for you when you

least expect it.

dissolve

negativity

DISSOLVE NEGATIVITY. MOVE TOWARDS EMOTIONAL NEUTRALITY. SOMETIMES BEING VULNERABLE OR OPEN CAN MAKE YOU STRONG. BEING REALLY TRUTHFUL WITH YOURSELF AND ADMITTING YOUR REAL FEELINGS WILL HELP YOU LET NEGATIVE EMOTIONS GO. THEN YOU CAN MOVE INTO AN EMOTIONALLY NEUTRAL POSITION ON ONCE AGAIN.

INDIFFERENCE

It is often said that the opposite to love is not hate – it's indifference. Transmuted as such, indifference can be one of your most powerful tools.

There may be times when you feel that your emotions are too overwhelming to be put on display, and occasionally a situation calls for more dignity. Indifference can provide a shield of privacy behind which you are able to process your *real* emotions. It will give you an aura of dignity in a difficult situation, while allowing you to be true to your real feelings.

You'll need to perfect a 'poker face', though, to carry it off!

153

Change the soundtrack!

Music can be a heavy nostalgia vehicle – for good or bad trips. Don't be a masochist and play music from times in your life when you've been hurt or depressed: it may be painful to hear and the lyrics may affect you in ways you're not even aware of.

Get some better emotions: put on something you love and that you know puts you in a great mood.

To move into a new phase, change up the vibe or to simply be inspired; get some new music. Tune into a radio station you wouldn't normally listen to and experiment with different kinds of music.

Or, for a change, try a meditation or motivational tape. Either will put you in a whole new frame of mind.

Sound is an important tool for healing. It can educate your ears, raise your energies, inspire you, relieve your anxieties and – best of all – transport you to another world.

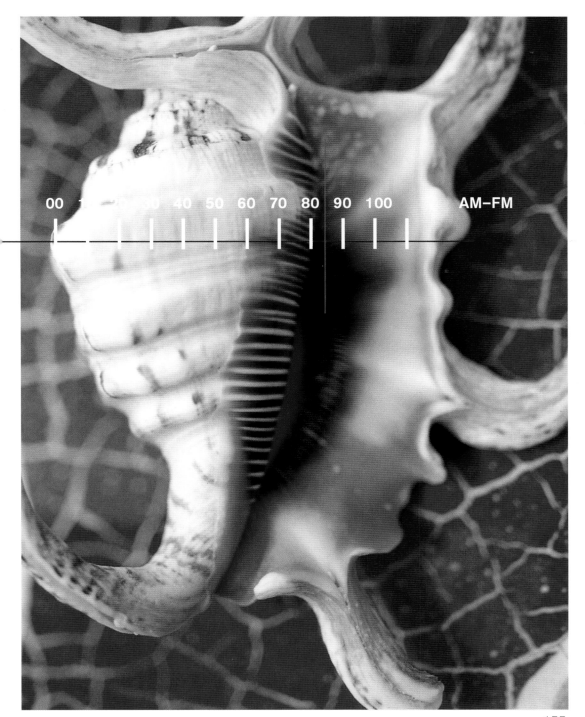

00   10   20   30   40   50   60   70   80   90   100   AM–FM

THERE ARE NO LIMITS

everyone

LIMITS

Melina, Peru

has a past...

but it's all behind you . . . NOW

believe in magic,

you walk in it.

energy: [def:n] Internal or inherent power, force, vigor; capability of action or performing work; active operation; a dynamic, changeable quality.

ene

explode

neurosis

end

[chakra: solar plexus chakra; integration of 'being', personality aligns with spiritual and earthly planes]

r*gy

repression   generate   yourself

pure

energy

it's all you need

fix it
ditch it
use it
run it
deal with it
get over it
get used to it
reject it
give up on it
dream it
do it
feel it
sing it
write it
create it
give to it
jump to it
come through it
hope for it
take to it
run over it
leave it
see it
trust in it
live it
make it
wipe it
forsake it
skip it
love it!

TAKE

ACTION!

Get EQUIPPED
KNOW stuff
Read BETWEEN
the lines
Stay abreast
VIEW up close
and from afar
QUESTION
EverYthinG

Be PERSISTENT

THINK.

Prayer beads, Tibet

If you can imagine it, you can have it.

Fertility statue, Africa

168

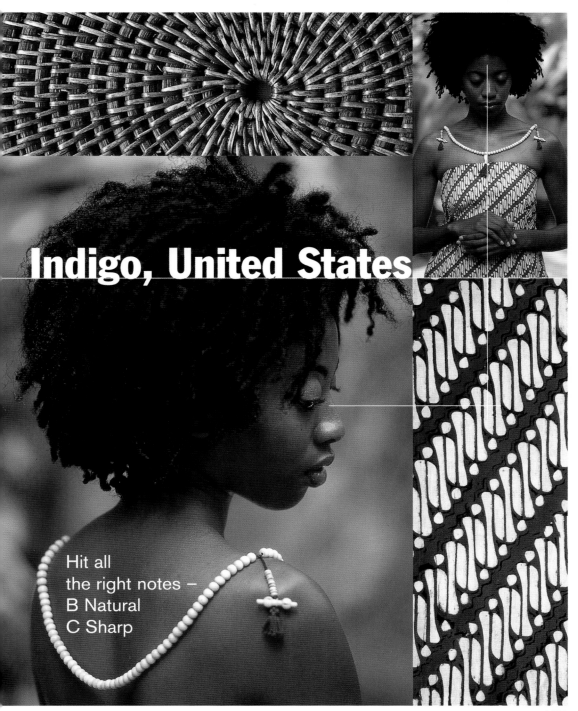

Indigo, United States

Hit all
the right notes –
B Natural
C Sharp

Choice –
it's a beautiful thing

Be decisive. Act powerfully. Make a decision and put energy, belief and pure intention behind it.

Choose to leave a bad relationship, an unsatisfying dead-end job or a negative living arrangement (like the roommate from hell!).

Choose to deserve all that is wonderful.

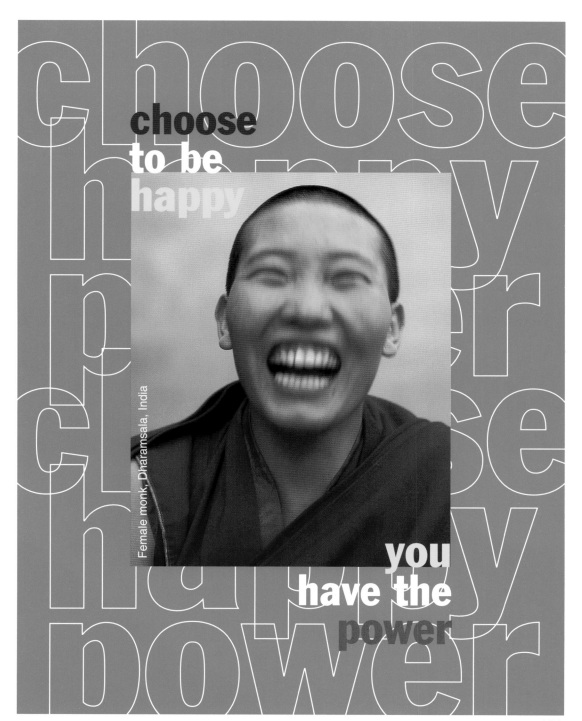

choose
to be
happy

Female monk, Dharamsala, India

you
have the
power

171

Clean
up
your
act...

Edit
your
life.

Keep
what
is
useful
important
beautiful.

Get
rid
of
the
rest.

Sometimes the Universe delivers a body blow in the form of an unexpected event that is a direct uppercut to your equilibrium: you lose your job, or your partner leaves out of the blue, or someone you depend on decides to move to Zanzibar. But instead of panicking, take a deep breath – then breathe out a huge sigh of relief! You probably had a gut feeling about it anyway, because the energy of the place or situation was beginning to expire. Now it's time to re-energize and begin a new phase – and you can design it however you want! It's time to take charge of your life and be thrilled that you now have the personal power to change anything that you want. You can reinvent yourself, so get busy – change, create, design, take charge!

CONFLICT – TIME TO TAKE THE GLOVES OFF!

Don't shy away from confrontation or conflict. Like the muscles in your body, which won't grow or stay toned and ready for action without pressure and a bit of pain, your spirit needs conflict in order to transcend.

As you grow stronger in your spirit and your confidence, it will be harder for people to manipulate or intimidate you. This may mean you'll have to deal with other forms of aggression, possibly even open hostility. Don't be afraid! You have an agenda and so do they, but people's agendas don't always mesh. If you find you need to defend your agenda, defend it!

You don't have to try and please everyone. Anyway, it's simply not possible.

KEEP YOUR BALANCE

KEEP YOUR COOL

KEEP YOUR

RELAX!

GO FOR A LONG WALK ● TAKE A TEA BREAK ● UNWIND IN A BATH ● PLAY WITH A DOG ● MEDITATE ● SIT ON A BEACH AND WATCH WAVES ● READ A BOOK ● ENJOY A TRASHY TV SHOW ● LAUGH WITH FRIENDS ● LAUGH ALONE ● WRITE TO SOMEONE YOU LOVE ● COOK YOUR FAVORITE RECIPE ● DRAW WHAT YOU SEE ● SIT IN A PARK ● ENJOY AN OLD MOVIE ● WORK IN THE GARDEN ● PLAY SOLITAIRE ● SLEEP ● PUT ON YOUR HEADPHONES AND ZONE OUT

FUN COSTS NOTHING, IS AVAILABLE 24–7 AND IS CENTRAL TO EVERYTHING.

DIG YOUR OWN GROOVE

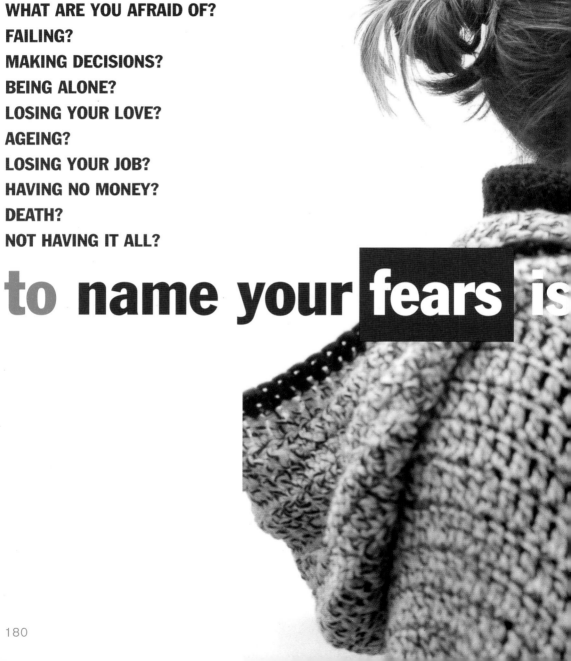

WHAT ARE YOU AFRAID OF?
FAILING?
MAKING DECISIONS?
BEING ALONE?
LOSING YOUR LOVE?
AGEING?
LOSING YOUR JOB?
HAVING NO MONEY?
DEATH?
NOT HAVING IT ALL?

to name your fears is

**TURN IT AROUND –
transmute fear to energy.
Think positive.
You could be –**

to DESTROY them.

Starting over.

Making another decision.

Living peacefully alone.

Finding new love.

Accepting change.

Beginning a new career.

Living more frugally, harmoniously, graciously.

Understanding life and the infinity of the spirit.

Moving forward to a new phase.

To sleep, perchance to dream . . .
William Shakespeare, *A Midsummer Night's Dream*

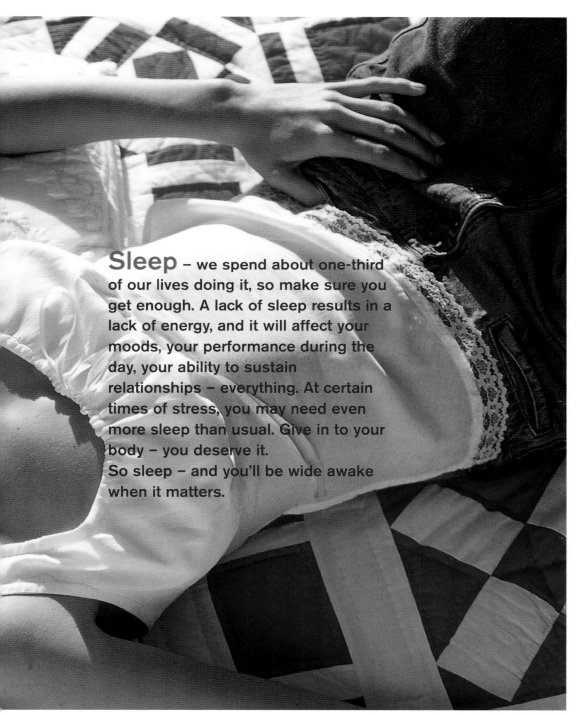

Sleep – we spend about one-third of our lives doing it, so make sure you get enough. A lack of sleep results in a lack of energy, and it will affect your moods, your performance during the day, your ability to sustain relationships – everything. At certain times of stress, you may need even more sleep than usual. Give in to your body – you deserve it.
So sleep – and you'll be wide awake when it matters.

BE

amusing
bright
original
sharp
inventive
optimistic
remarkable
charming
pure
imaginative
forgiving
genuine
irrepressible
honest
fascinating
interested
tolerant
consistent
passionate
sensitive
observant
patient
kind
respected
happy
light
respectful
generous
interesting
loyal
able
instinctive
loving
positive
compassionate
candid

REAL

Natalie, France

Add
fuel
for
more
fire.

Paradox

Life's like that.
To get energy, you need to
expend energy.
The more you do, the more you
can do.
To get the most out of life, you need
to get into it.
To receive love you need to give it.
In taking no risks you are really risking
everything.

awareness: [def:n] To be conscious and have
knowledge of one's existence and form; having immediate knowledge, to be
awake in a metaphysical way; with one's senses alive and possessing a fine-
tuned perception of detail; the essential ingredient for a spiritual life.

awar

another   world   awakens   reality   exp eness

esses   nature   essence   spirit   soars

s p i r i t

your breath

is the

only connection

between you

and the

outside world

b r e a t h i n g

Pay attention and it will pay you back!

192

Savoir faire – to know, to do

Increasingly, life will throw up extraordinary scenarios that require greater adeptness and higher levels of skills than previous experiences required.

So it's in your best interest to actively seek to gain the knowledge, poise and maturity that you may be called upon to demonstrate in the future.

You need savoir faire. Savoir faire is a grace and ability to harmonize that will carry you through any event that life dishes up. It is most often learned through observing other people – sometimes if only to learn what not to do. So when someone acts badly, imagine how you might change the outcome by acting out the parts in your mind. Imagine the outcome of a difficult situation where no one loses face, and where everyone walks away a winner. Savoir faire is the inner voice that helps us to do the right thing, at the right time, for the highest good of all concerned.

tune out. turn off.

drop in ... to consciousness.

Process your thoughts –
Meditation is the key.

Cut through thought to consciousness.

See yourself sitting behind a waterfall of thoughts. Let it flow. What is the thought behind the thought? Can you see behind someone else's thought? Is the essence of the thought pure? If not, reject it outright. Let it fall away into the pool below.

Move away from negativity. Move towards the positives. Recognize that each of these forces has a role to play in helping you to grow and manifest things in your life for the better. One does not exist without the other. There can be no light without darkness, and there is always an opportunity for growth and awareness, no matter what.

Awareness grows in silence. This is where your spirit takes shape.

Meditation - train your brain

To control the mind and not be ruled by aimless or unfocused 'thought drift' is a challenge for almost everyone. Too much mental activity can cause stress, and when this is added to the pressures of life you can end up feeling like you're on an emotional rollercoaster. With so much information and thought from external sources coming into our conscious minds, there is more than ever a need to stem the influx and reduce stress.

Happily, you can help reduce stress through meditation. Meditation is an ancient practise that aims – through deep concentration, breath observation and relaxation of the conscious mind – to reach a state of calmness and 'thoughtlessness' that lies between consciousness and deep sleep.

By training your mind to be still, meditation also allows you to go beyond thought to an awareness of the *real* you. Modern living can be savage and you may feel a weird sense of being disconnected from your true self. Meditation reconnects you to your spirit and is essential for your ongoing development and for understanding who you are and who you might become.

It's not a competition, though. Meditation is an intensely personal, private and individual thing. No two minds are the same and therefore no one's meditation is like another's.

There are many different ways to meditate. You could learn it in a course or from a book, but the easiest method is breath observation. Breathe through your nose with your mouth closed. Your eyes can either be closed or half open. Your body can be in any position, but it is sometimes better to be sitting because it's all too easy to drop off to sleep if you are lying down! Go with whatever is comfortable. Use a cushion on the floor if you need to or sit on a chair with your feet flat on the floor.

Then, once you are ready, begin to breathe. Listen to your breathing and let go any thoughts that arise as you gently return to your focus on your breath. Don't follow any train of thought; gently return to the rise and fall of your breath.

Do it for as long as you can. It may be just a few minutes to start with, and then you may work up to longer periods. Some people use an alarm clock; others do it until they feel like looking at their watches. It's a personal choice. But try to do it regularly.

A little meditation goes a long way.

WHAT ARE YOU PUTTING INTO YOUR MIND?
WHAT ARE YOU ALLOWING TO GO IN?

Be selective about what your mind receives, because once it's there, even if it's only a momentary impression, it is stored in some form and will affect your thought processes. Choose television programs, movies, radio and reading material carefully. You can control what you take in – and you should.

Limit your exposure.

Self-censorship allows you to control what goes into your mind.

Remember – you're the boss!

It's part of looking after yourself: mind, body and soul.

LIMIT YOUR EXPOSURE

desires
wants
reactions

It's human nature . . .

Desire begins in the mind.
Wants and fears govern reactions.

We desire and fear in proportion to the intensity of the thoughts that we have mentally cultivated throughout our lives. The secret is not to *want* too much, as often the attachment to an outcome of 'having' is really the fear, in disguise, of 'not having' the object of your desire. However, this ego-attachment will push the very thing further away that you most desire. It is the fear of not having that drives the state of wanting, and anything based on this fear will generate a negative result.

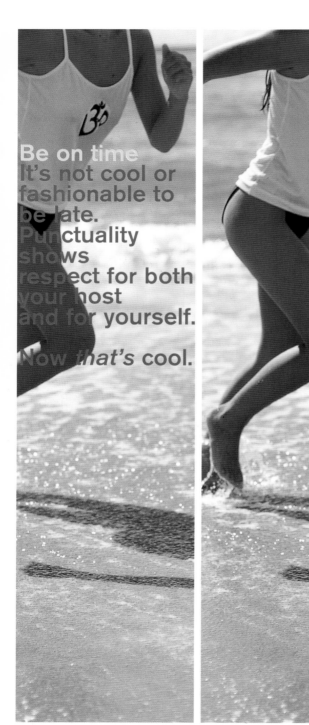

Be on time
It's not cool or
fashionable to
be late.
Punctuality
shows
respect for both
your host
and for yourself.

Now *that's* cool.

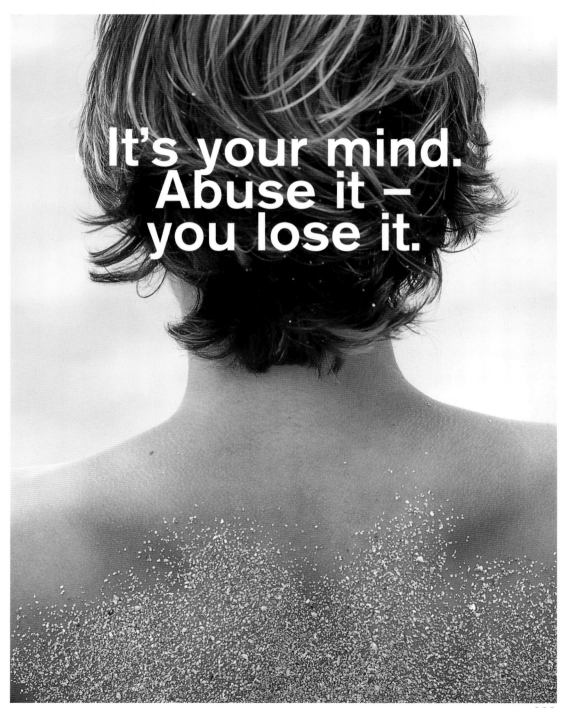

It's your mind.
Abuse it –
you lose it.

trust your intuition

basic instincts

give yourself a hand

People will do basically what they want to do. So let them. Don't manipulate or try to change other people, especially for your own advantage.

Live and LET LIVE.
Flow and LET FLOW.

It doesn't mean you have to always give in to other people, but step back to see if something is really what you want, or just what you *say* you want!

Follow your INSTINCTS. If you push away your intuition – which is there to help you – things tend to blow up in your face later!

Give yourself a hand – TRUST YOUR INTUITION.

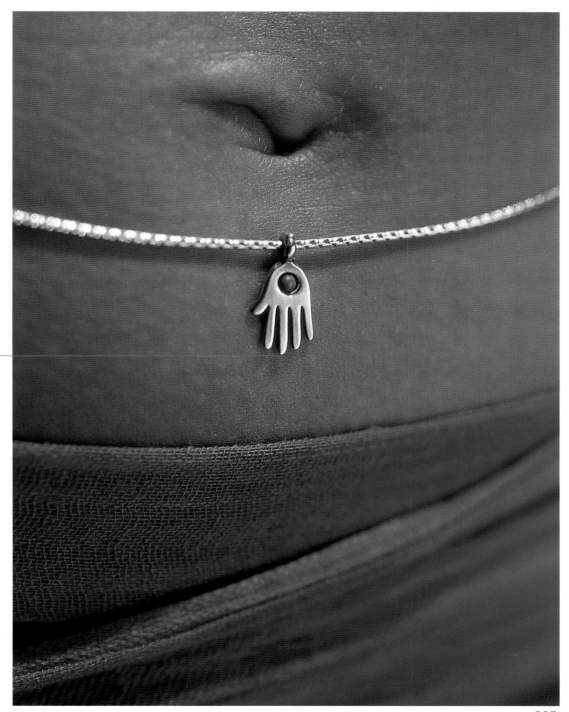

Sometimes knowing when to let go of something or how to stop manipulating a situation is extremely difficult. It can be one of the toughest tests that life can present.

We all face such turning points in our lives, but by recognizing them, acting fluidly and in accordance with universal laws, rather than resisting and reacting, we are being offered the ultimate opportunity.

In fact, there are patterns in everything – you just need to recognize them when they occur. So each time a situation arises the universe is giving you another chance to get it right and move on, up to the next level. You can either ignore the clues and be stuck in a cycle or you can change your attitude, behavior and reactions to transcend it.

The only way you'll get it right is by objectively reviewing and learning from your mistakes. What are the facts? Who else was involved? What was your contribution? Don't judge, but try to draw some conclusions that will help you in the future. Soon you'll be an expert in recognizing all the signs. When you can bypass a situation you'll know you've graduated. After all, the best education is the one you give yourself through experience and 'a sign is only meaningful if you know how to interpret it' (Arthur Golding, *Memoirs of a Geisha*).

life's education.
sometimes it's the school of hard knocks
(BUT AT LEAST IT'S AN EDUCATION FOR LIFE)

breathe
breathe
breathe
breathe
breathe
breathe
breathe
breathe
breathe
breathe
breathe
breathe
breathe
breathe
breathe
breathe
breathe
breathe
breathe
breathe
breathe
breathe
breathe
breathe
breathe
breathe
breathe
breathe
breathe . . . just breathe

Are you in the funhouse?

Take a reality check: everything around you is a reflection of the energy you're

giving out, but from time to time you

could be confused by the image of

yourself that you're receiving.

Sometimes the reflection you get

back from others is distorted – it's like

you're in the Hall of Mirrors in an

amusement park. Bear in mind that

each image only tells part of the story,

so it's up to you to decide how much of another's opinion (and it's often only

an *opinion*) is truthful and accurate, and therefore how much adjustment, if

any, you should make.

THE THIRD EYE There are many ways of seeing. After all, reality is perception, and everyone sees reality differently. Try going beyond the obvious and the ephemeral to *feel* reality instead. If you can free the clutter from your mind, you will liberate your perception from its ego-based prejudices. Let your soul do the seeing and you will see reality with the eye in your heart, not the eyes in your head.

WAYS OF SEEING

'open your eyes and look within...
are you satisfied with the life you're living?'

BOB MARLEY, 'EXODUS'

EYES WIDE OPEN

silent

212

p o w e r

Statue, Bali, Indonesia

Sometimes the best thing to say is – nothing at all.
SILENCE is POWERFUL when you use it to strengthen your position.
Find power in silence. *Feel* the answer to something rather than listen to it.
The true answer is often the one you feel, *not* the one you hear.

LISTEN CAREFULLY

WATCH FOR THE SIGNS

LISTEN TO THE WIND

TO YOUR INSTINCTS

TO YOUR HEART

listen

When you are talking to someone, be with them fully, focused on what is being said, not with what's going on in your head.

This is called listening.

Listening is not passive. It's an active part of dialogue and it works both ways.

The winds of change blow freely and constantly, but only for those who can hear.

growth: [def:n] The ongoing results of the act or
process of growing; an increase in number, power or degree due to the
assimilation of new matter into a living organism, development, change in
form and substance, cultivation of the essential being, the production of a
result, the passing from one state to another, to advance to maturity and
understanding. The process of developing roots by which to gather nutrients
to aid further intrinsic growth.

gro

germinate   reap   offer

[chakra: throat chakra; relates to communication of emotions and regulates transition of the self towards inward reflection]

w t h

water   tend   honor

WHO are YOU?

If you want to be someone, be yourself.

get your own gig
other people's expectations = pressure

take the heat off –
run your own race!

SELF-RELIANCE

YOUR CHOOSING

Total self-reliance is the best way.

Develop SELF-RELIANCE as a habit that is second nature.

Then, if or when there is a time that you need to take refuge and be dependent, surrender comes as a blissful alternative, and something of YOUR CHOOSING.

224

DISCIPLINE

WILLPOWER

Discipline. Do you have what it takes?
DISCIPLINE is knowing deep down who you are and what your VALUES are.
Discipline is supporting that knowledge with action and the necessary
organisation to follow through. Discipline is the behavior that totally reflects
those values and, through continuous exertion of WILLPOWER, enables them
to have expression in every facet of your life.

Had it.

Lost it.

THE UNWILLINGNESS TO BE RESPONSIBLY SELFISH = SELF-SABOTAGE

EXPRESS

YOURSELF!

Find the little quirks in your own personality and enjoy them. Use them to DEFINE yourself. Don't become cloned or let anyone tell you how they like you or how you should be. That's unoriginal and *you're not*.

You are completely ORIGINAL. There has never existed in history a person like you. Ever. Do not underestimate the importance of your uniqueness. Find and develop your own vibe; don't borrow it from someone else. Seek out new people if the ones around you don't bring out the best in you and allow you to be yourself. You are, above all, an individual.
So be one!

Learn to be alone – it makes you grow

loneliness is a state of mind

Everyone feels lonely at some time, and everyone is alone at some time.

The difference lies in how each one of us reacts to it when it happens.

There are many ways of filling ourselves up, say, with activities or people,

 but a lot of the time we spend our time less well than we should, doing

things we'd rather not or being with people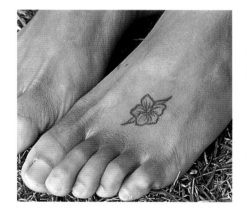

who, in our hearts, we care little for. But

because we are frightened to be on our

own, we compromise.

Being alone is not a badge of disgrace – it

is a precious and beautiful thing. So

welcome solitude, enjoy each moment, as if

you may never be alone again. Turn it into a positive time. Create a dream

project – actually do something about it – and soon you'll be guarding your

privacy and your space.

In reality we are all alone, but at least we're all in it together. For loneliness is

nothing, and once overcome, the achievement and satisfaction is greater than

anything you can imagine.

'what do you hang

on the walls of your mind?

EVE ARNOLD, PHOTOGRAPHER

What are your treasured images from years of seeing? What are the pictures that line your memory bank, stored as a result of absorbing the world around you?

There might be a picture or pictures taken of you as a child, or one taken of your parents when they were first married. Perhaps there is an image that you once tore out of a magazine or the odd postcard from a far-flung place. Each of these images can evoke pleasure, pain, peace or a myriad of other emotions.

Like images in an art gallery you can revisit these images over time and see them anew. For while a picture may remain the same, your perception of it will change as you change.

It is wise therefore to review the images you have mentally stored and to edit, affirm, replace and/or revitalize those that no longer have any relevance or that cause pain.

in your memory bank…

Incense sticks, Tibet

Be ruthless: if you are storing up negative images, they can be harmful in the long term. And constantly seek to find new imagery to stimulate your creativity. Your mind will repay you in a thousand different ways and new images will allow you to keep moving forward on your adventure through life.

Seek ways to record those visual experiences that capture your attention. Keeping a scrapbook can be a wonderful way to reflect on your journey, and to mark turning points in your life that may not be obvious until years later.

In order to move forward, you must make peace with, and release, the past. In order to have a full life, you must constantly let go of things and create new space for more fullness.

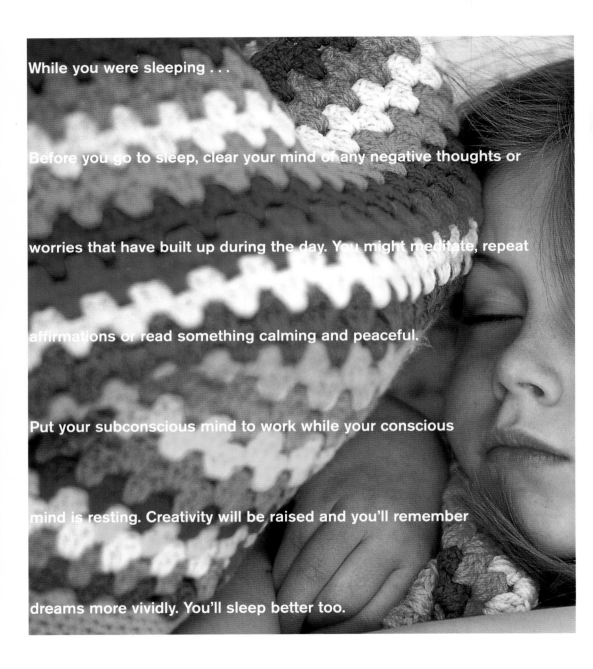

While you were sleeping . . .

Before you go to sleep, clear your mind of any negative thoughts or

worries that have built up during the day. You might meditate, repeat

affirmations or read something calming and peaceful.

Put your subconscious mind to work while your conscious

mind is resting. Creativity will be raised and you'll remember

dreams more vividly. You'll sleep better too.

DREAMS ARE REAL TOO . . .
WHAT ARE YOUR DREAMS
TELLING YOU?
THEY MAY HOLD THE KEY TO
UNDERSTANDING THE
MYSTERY OF LIFE ITSELF. CARL
JUNG AND SIGMUND FREUD
THE FOUNDERS OF MODERN
PSYCHOLOGY, CERTAINLY
THOUGHT SO. THEY BELIEVED
THAT SELF-ANALYSIS CAN BE
GREATLY ASSISTED BY SIFTING
THROUGH DREAM IMAGERY
AND SYMBOLISM.
KEEP A DREAM JOURNAL OF
YOUR NIGHTLY SUBCONSCIOUS
ESCAPADES. IT CAN BE AN
EXCELLENT TOOL FOR
UNDERSTANDING YOURSELF
AND FOR CHANGING PATTERNS
OF BEHAVIOR.

open the doors of perception

THE BEST EDUCATION IS THE ONE
YOU GIVE YOURSELF.

APOLOGIES: WHO AND WHAT ARE YOU SORRY FOR?

Shadow boxing – fighting the demons within

Fear is your motivator and your friend. By facing fear, whether it is fear of failure, fear of losing something or someone – even fear of success – it loses it's power over you. There is an old saying that you have nothing to fear but fear itself. Fear will paralyse you, if you allow it.

Don't let your fear get the better of you! It's a mind game, and you're in control of your mind. Use fear to motivate and inspire you. Treat it as an ally. Make peace with it. Accept that it is there and allow it to have a role in spurring you on – onwards and upwards!

Sometimes life gives you exactly what you are fearful of, to teach you, through direct experience, how your fearful or negative thoughts can draw the precise thing to you that you most dreaded. So be strong, think positive, abundant thoughts and be confident that life will give you positive experiences. Eliminate and neutralize fearful situations by realising that you cannot be 'owned' by an illusion – because fear is just an illusion.

RESISTANCE – ARE YOU GETTING ANY?

1. HOLD EVERYTHING. STOP!
2. CONTROL YOUR MIND: REFUSE TO LET IT BECOME A NEGATIVE STRUGGLE.
3. THINK CAREFULLY: WHAT IS HAPPENING *EXACTLY?*
4. CHANGE TACK: MAYBE THERE'S RESISTANCE BECAUSE IT'S NOT THE RIGHT PATH. TRY ANOTHER ONE.
5. GO BACK TO BEING IN THE FLOW . . . LET THINGS TAKE THEIR NATURAL COURSE WITHOUT YOU DRIVING THEM SO HARD FOR A WHILE.
6. **HANG IN THERE UNTIL YOU'RE IN A RHYTHM AGAIN.**
7. NOW, CHILL OUT.
8. COOL? NOW YOU'VE GOT THE EMOTION OUT – WHAT'S LEFT?
9. CHECK OUT YOUR DESIRED GOAL AGAIN. NOW ARE YOU GETTING ANY RESISTANCE?

DON'T PRETEND.
KEEP IT REAL.
THE TRUTH
WILL ALWAYS
BE REVEALED.

CHANGE IS
PRETTY
INTENSE
GO EASY
ON
YOURSELF.

When you reach a point where you have it all together
(well, most of it at least)
or you consider you are a pretty good package
or you really have done the work on yourself
or you just feel you have gone to another level,
remember: just because you look like a one-stop shop,
it doesn't mean that you are now the 7–11,
open at anyone's convenience. Be discerning.
Check them out fully before you allow them to even browse.
Are they a real buyer or will they waste your time 'just looking'?

THE PRACTICAL GIRL AND THE SPIRITUAL GIRL — TOGETHER FOREVER.

MOVE TOWARDS THE POSITIVES. YOU GROW GIRL!

spirit: [def:n] The immaterial part of a person or being; the soul; a supernatural being; mental or moral force; real meaning or intent; pervading influence; to animate; the inner nature derived from or pertaining to a higher God-like force; pure; holy; sacred; divine; inspired; courageous; enlivened.

super   power   infinitely

[chakra: third eye chakra; the infinite spiritual intelligence passes through this chakra and by doing so affects and influences the individual as a whole]

rit

real   in   time

true beauty is the spirit within

Passion – the key ingredient for a beautiful life

Make it happen

Taj Mahal, Agra, India

The hungry spirit is a rebel with a cause. If you want to know the meaning of your life, you are going to have to design a higher purpose for it. The spirit within is hungry and you must feed it something more than mere existence for it to flourish. Believing in something and acting on that belief will nourish your soul. Contribute to the world and contribute to your own spiritual growth at the same time.

'sow a thought and reap an act,
sow an act and reap a habit,
sow a habit and reap a character,
sow a character and reap a destiny'

Quoted in Huston Smith, *The Religions of Man*

rebel : with a cause

SHINE ON

spirit lives

Your spirit is your essence.

It's also an aura that
surrounds you. It affects and
reflects the energy of all that
is you.

Be tuned to your aura.

Consciously let it shine.

Your spirit will take you to the
next level.

SHINE. **OM.**

KNOW TRUTH
SEEK TRUTH

The fields of truth
are the heartland of your soul.

let your spirit do the walking.

Death happens, not just to the physical body of someone or something, but to everything that comes to an end.

We are taught to be frightened of death, but death can be understood as a chance for renewal.

Death, loss and grief

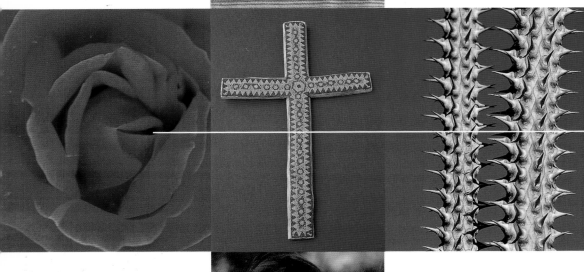

With death, new things are born or come into your life. If you believe in reincarnation or rebirth, then the death of the physical body can be viewed as a chance for the spirit to come again.

Whatever your beliefs, allow death to have its role and purpose. By accepting it you will learn how to let go and move forward. As well, you will understand the ebb and flow of the cycle that we are inextricably a part of: birth – life – growth – attachment – death – loss – grief – disengagement – rebirth.

Death and new beginnings are part of the evolution of your spirit. We need these lessons to grow up and out into the world. At the time it's very confusing, hurtful and painful and can make us bitter, angry and resentful. But we each have a duty to carry on living our life the way the Universe, God or the Spirit intended. Until it's our turn.

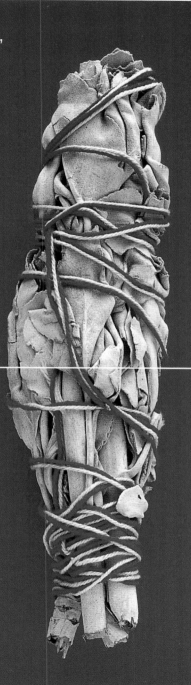

Smudge stick, Taos, New Mexico

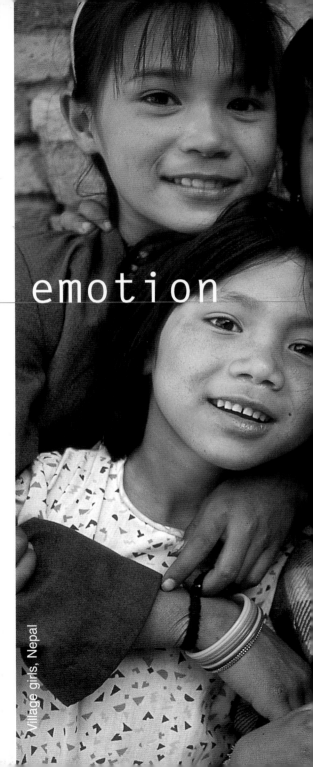

Show some emotion

Village girls, Nepal

We are the living composite of the Universe. We are part flower,

part shark and tiger, ape, tree, cloud, dog, part bird. We have it all within.

Any characteristic that you can see in nature, you will also find in yourself.

We are both predator and victim – one and the same – eternally. We are

not divided from that which would kill, hurt or love us. This is one of the

key universal truths. Look closely at yourself for then you'll understand

why you too can 'float like a butterfly, sting like a bee' (Muhammad Ali).

Bodhi tree, India

THE UNIVERSE WITHIN

U N I T Y =

creative power   physical mastery

SPIRITUAL STRENGTH

YOGA
mind control

= **THE LINK**

the path of the hungry spirit

THE POWER

O F   P R A Y E R

The power of prayer

Prayer is a valuable mechanism for reflection, the release of issues and for personal growth. Prayer allows you to develop a relationship with yourself and helps you understand Universal energies. It doesn't matter who or what you pray to — God, the Universe, Spirit, Buddha, Krishna, Allah — but inviting

the highest force to be a part of your life is powerful.

Like anything, the best results occur when you do it consistently and with a purity of intention. Through prayer you can heal (yourself and others), relieve anxiety, solve problems and change the things in your life that need changing. It allows you to 'clear channels', so you can be receptive to the right energies that you need, the ones that guide you to your spiritual evolution.

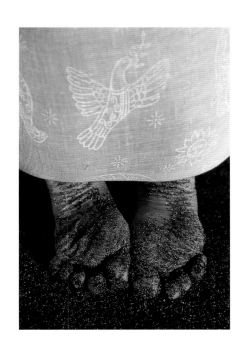

amen

You affect everyone and everything

Female monks, Dharamsala, India

You have two clear-cut choices in any situation: you can either positively affect it or negatively do so. You do it with words, actions or thoughts and the vibe that you bring with you – your energy.

Any chance to improve something or affect it in a positive way that is passed up is, by default, negative. It's easy to take the lazy option, but it will result in contributing nothing. So make the conscious effort to infuse positivity into every situation with your thoughts and your actions. Karma is organic.

Change your mind

cosmic

We never stand still, we are constant motion, all of us cosmic dancers. We are born to trip the light fantastic, to step and bow on the world stage, keeping our own perspectives but always in the context and in awareness of others. We are duty bound to act universally, for while we are each a child of our own culture, we must never lose sight of how closely related we are. Dance on in this knowledge for it is time to take another step, another leap into a future of love, curiosity, learning and pride in the whole of humankind and the vast experience that is our common legacy.

dancer

jiva

the individual soul

you are not your body

you are not your mind

you are the eternal spirit

this you must know . . .

Crystal bowl ceremony, Bali

connect with the spirit – the universal power that created you – for this is how you will find the meaning of your life. it guides you to the highest good for your spiritual evolution.

Village girls, Thar Desert, India

'The **spirit** within you is a river. Its sacred bathing place is contemplation; Its waters are **truth;** Its banks are **holiness;** Its waves are love. Go to that river for purification: your soul cannot be made pure by mere water.'

Extract from the Hitopadesa
(Sanskrit stories, India)

sacred spirit

KEEP YOUR HEART AS PURE AS A TEMPLE BELL

Temple monkey, Nepal

TRANSCEND YOUR LIFE

LIVE IT TO THE MAX

hope : [def:n] An expectant desire; a confidence in a future event; a ground for trust and confidence; to think; to look forward to with trust and expectant desire.

heaven

opens

[chakra: crown chakra; the individual experiences totality and a connection to the Universe beyond the confines of intellect merging with the pure consciousness of the Divine]

personal   expression

TODAY IS THE TOMORROW YOU WERE DREAMING OF YESTERDAY.

DREAM
DREAM
DREAM
DREAM

DREAM
DREAM
DREAM

DREAM

DREAM

DREAM

DREAM

DREAM

DREAM

It doesn't matter where you've been, you can still change where you're going.

Hope is a driving factor in helping us stay on course in life. It may feel as though it comes and goes, but in reality there is always hope. There is always a chance for something else to happen, and you need to have faith that it will.

Hope is the last word.

Daily affirmation

I love and trust myself in every way and I accept myself without judging

because I am part of the Universe, created of and by the infinite being.

I can manifest all of my dreams and desires because I have a personal

connection to the infinite intelligence and I am at one with this power.

It is possible for me to exceed my goals because beauty, power and harmony

abound in my heart and in my mind.

I am able to love, forgive and release everything in the past.

I am able to attract as many positive experiences as I want and need and

recognize this as part of my individual destiny.

I believe in the unlimited peace and love which, as a child of the Universe,

is my birthright.

Is your cup
half full or
half empty?
you *decide*.

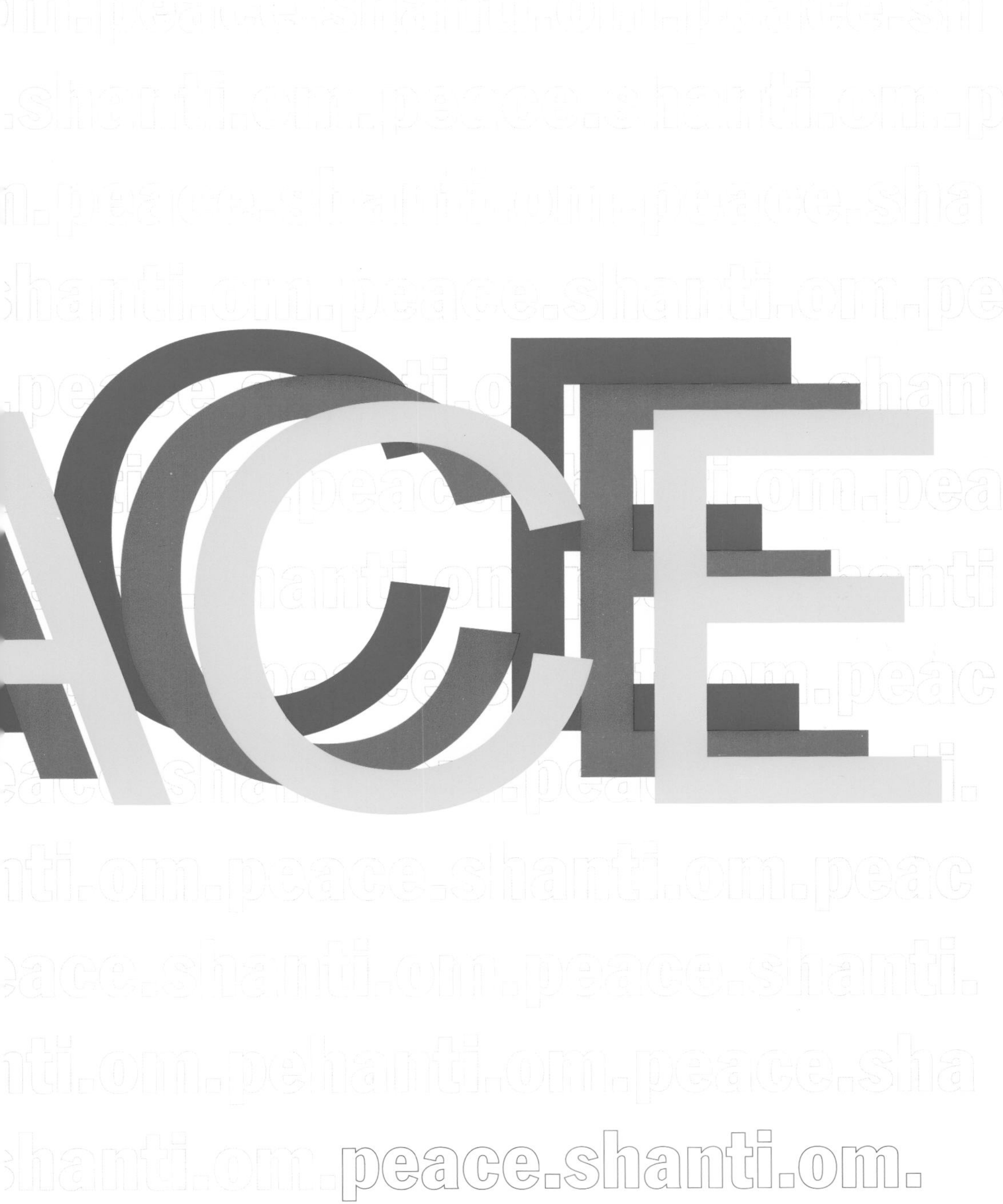
peace.shanti.om.

Every day is a new:
beginning
chance
challenge
battle
?
Your
choice.

Beginning anything is always nerve-wracking,
endings are often sad,
and frequently heart-rending,
and there will be many throughout your life.
But in truth it's the part in between,
what happened there and what you did there,
that really counts.

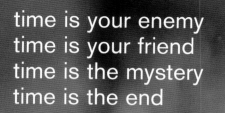

time is your enemy
time is your friend
time is the mystery
time is the end

Divide your time 24–7:
8 hours' work
8 hours' play
8 hours' sleep

'listen and be inspired because in everything you see, hear and do, there is a gift'

Pablita Velarde, painter, New Mexico

count your blessings

PAST IMPERFECT AND PRESENT TENSE?
RELAX — YOUR FUTURE IS AHEAD OF YOU AND YOU CAN
START AGAIN ANY TIME YOU WANT. YOU DO HAVE TO
WANT IT, THOUGH, AND

THE FUTURE IS NOW.

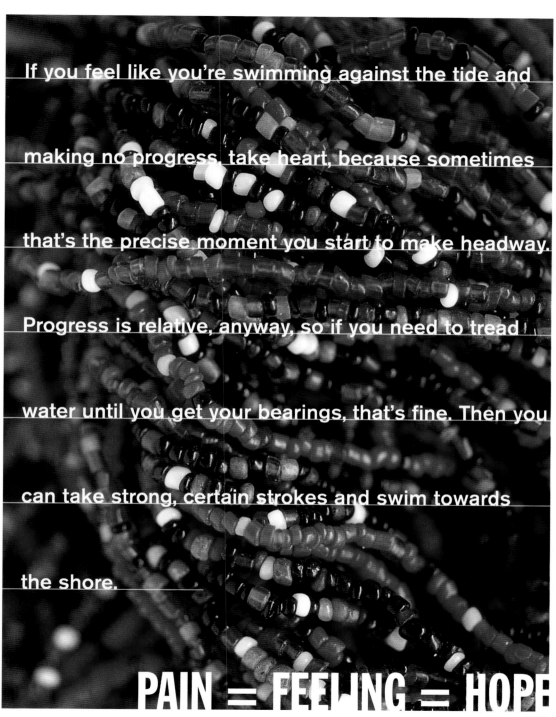

If you feel like you're swimming against the tide and

making no progress, take heart, because sometimes

that's the precise moment you start to make headway.

Progress is relative, anyway, so if you need to tread

water until you get your bearings, that's fine. Then you

can take strong, certain strokes and swim towards

the shore.

PAIN = FEELING = HOPE

Look after your inner child –
she is pure innocence.

Each one of us has the potential to make a positive contribution to the world. It is our responsibility to do what we can while we're here. Native Americans believe that while on earth people should leave no trace, and it is true that we should all endeavor to leave as little mess or pollution as possible while we are here on the earthly plane. But we should try and leave our spirit behind, in the form of positivity and a kindness remembered. This is passed on by helping in whatever capacity we can to improve the lives of others.

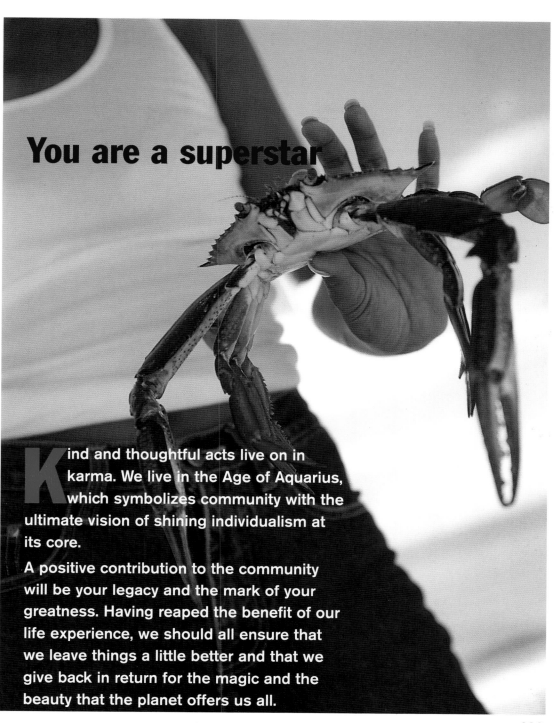

You are a superstar

Kind and thoughtful acts live on in karma. We live in the Age of Aquarius, which symbolizes community with the ultimate vision of shining individualism at its core.

A positive contribution to the community will be your legacy and the mark of your greatness. Having reaped the benefit of our life experience, we should all ensure that we leave things a little better and that we give back in return for the magic and the beauty that the planet offers us all.

Astral traveler

You are on a voyage in space, time and eternity. On the earthly plane –

the third dimension – you may feel weighed down by your own physical

limitations, and this feeling manifests as

insecurities and fears. But this is just an illusion

of form over function – your soul is on a

perpetual discovery mission and forever is

a very long time.

So relax and enjoy the trip. You are, above all,

an adventurer in the cosmos, limitless,

boundless and multidimensional.

It's your individual quest that you need to honor.

You have nothing to fear anymore. There is no more pain.

There is no more need for insecurity. There is only possibility.

Believe it and there will be no constraints to your journey.

You go, cosmic girl.

Angels are watching . . .

THERE ARE NO FIXED OUTCOMES

CHANGE IS ALWAYS POSSIBLE.

don't look back

your future's right in front of you

FACE
THE FUTURE

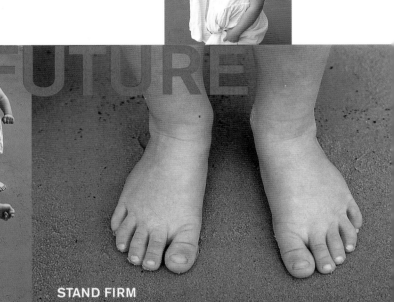

STAND FIRM

PLAY ALONG

BE POSITIVE

THE BEST
IS YET TO COME

STICK TOGETHER

woman: [def:n] An adult female human; womankind; the female gender.

wor

wise original mag

[chakra: crown chakra; absolute and total connection with the Universe, the limitations of the self are overcome by the merging of cosmic energies with pure consciousness]

ical   angel   now

A TOUGH VULNERABILITY.
AN ORNATE SIMPLICITY.
A RUTHLESS COMPASSION.
SENSUAL.WARM.AWARE.
CALM.HOPEFUL.WISE.
ACCEPTING.REJECTING.
GROWN.WARY.GENUINE.
SELECTIVE.ACTIVE.RESTING.
BALANCED.EDGY.SPIRITUAL.
VIRTUAL.DIMENSIONAL.
SURREAL.REAL.DIRECTIONAL.
UNCHARTED.CHARTED.
FESTIVE.TACTILE.
MOTIVATED.WOVEN.DESIRING.
CHALLENGING.FOCUSED.
REALIZED.FULFILLED.
SEASONED.INFINITE.
DECIDED.TRANQUIL.HAPPY.
FLUID.ORGANIC.REFLECTIVE.
ANTICIPATORY.CONSCIOUS.
CELEBRATORY.ALIVE.
ETERNAL...

woman

Girlossary

ABSOLUTE – independent, unlimited, under no restraint; self-existent; highly accomplished, perfect; unconditioned; existing independently of any other cause.

ARTIFICIAL – made or produced by art; not natural, not real; affected in manner; feigned.

BEAUTY CULTURE – improvement of women's appearance by artificial and unnatural means.

BUDDHA – a being who is fully enlightened; derived from the Sanskrit origin 'budh' meaning to be aware of, conscious or awakened.

CHAKRA – a Sanskrit word meaning 'wheel of light'. Sometimes referred to as 'gateways to consciousness', chakras are also known as energy centers within the etheric body which are in constant rotation. Traditionally there are seven chakras: crown, third eye, throat, heart, solar plexus, lower abdomen and root. Each chakra is associated with a specific region of the body as each has its own purpose and is a source for healing therapy. When chakras are out of balance, healing is required. Rebalancing the chakras restores vitality as well as unity to the chakras' combined functioning. Mantras and tones as well as massage can be applied to each chakra for healing. Ultimately, having and maintaining one's chakras in balance means that the individual soul can be united (or reunited) with the Collective Universal Soul.

DESTINY – our individual future as designed by our own efforts in combination with our past and present karma. Destiny is created and changed by acting with free will.

DIVINE – pertaining to, proceeding from or of the nature of a god or gods; sacred, above the nature of man; superhuman, god-like, celestial; the quality of perfection, excellence.

ENLIGHTENMENT – the highest level of awareness, understanding and unity with the truth of all things; of being in 'oneness' with consciousness.

FEMINISM – a movement advocating equal material, economic, social and spiritual rights for women.

FENG SHUI – a traditional Chinese philosophy that teaches us to understand the principal energies (yin and yang) of the Universe and to live so that we do not disturb their harmony and flow. It is an art (literally meaning 'wind' and 'water') of bringing into balance and harmony the flow of natural energies, in particular the essential life force ('ch'i') through cleansing, clearing and beautifying one's personal space and the arrangement and placement of objects. The philosophy is based on the understanding of the duality of life as represented by the forces of yin and yang. Theirs is a constant energy exchange, which we in life are always trying to balance.

INCENSE AND SMUDGE STICKS – used to cleanse auras and raise the vibrational level and quality of atmospheres. Smudge sticks are made from a combination of herbs such as sage, pine or cedar and are used in Native American traditional rituals and ceremonies.

JIVA – an individual soul.

KARMA – a Sanskrit term meaning action or deed. Any physical or mental action is karma. All of our acts or karma throughout our lives result in our destiny.

MANDALA – a diagram, often circular, of the cosmos, representing the individual in wholeness and in perfect harmony with the rest of the Universe. The concentric nature of the symbol, which is used as an aid to meditation practise, is suggestive of the individual's passage from the material state to the spiritual, or the journey of the soul from the periphery of existence to the core of all understanding. At the center is unity and eternity and at the periphery is perfection.

MANTRA – a chant ('om mane padme hum' or, simply, 'om') to be intoned repeatedly as an aid and focus in meditation practise.

MEDITATION – a state or realm between consciousness and sleep as entered by an individual upon the practise of breath observation and deep concentration; training the mind to be still through breath control with the aim of increasing 'awareness'; deep thought and mental focus.

METAPHYSICAL – literally, 'after' or 'beyond' the physical. Metaphysics is the philosophy of being and knowing as in thought, beyond the physical signs that can be observed. It is transcendental.

NATURAL – of, pertaining to, produced, or constituted by nature; innate, inherent, uncultivated, not artificial; inborn, instinctive; in conformity with the ordinary course of nature; true to life; unaffected, not forced or exaggerated; undisguised; to be expected.

OM – the universal word and symbol, 'om' is 'thought' in the Buddhist tradition. It is the representation of the universal sound when chanted and is symbolically comprised of four components: the three sections, which are underneath the half-moon shape representing the piercing of the veil to the circle (top), and the attainment of enlightenment being the achievement of pure consciousness.

REAL – actually existing; not affected; true, genuine; not counterfeit, but of substance; having an absolute and independent existence; that which is actual as opposed to the ideal; the genuine thing.

SAMSARA – the continuous cycle of birth, death and rebirth; from the Sanskrit word meaning 'passing through intensely' in relation to the process by which a 'jiva' or individual soul passes through a sequence of bodies; reincarnation; the transmigration of the soul.

SOUL – the essential eternal being and the blueprint for immortality; the spiritual part of a person or being.

STEREOTYPE – to fix or establish in unchangeable form.

TALISMAN – a charm, an amulet or a magical figure to which specific powers, effects and benefits can be ascribed. For example, talismans worn on the body as jewelry can contain crystals that have certain properties for healing and protection.

TRANSCEND – to rise above, surpass, excel, exceed, pass through or be beyond the range, sphere or power (of human understanding, physical experience etc.).

TRUTH – the state or quality of being true; conformity to fact or ultimate reality; that which is true; honesty, sincerity, fidelity, constancy.

ZEN – from the Japanese Buddhist tradition, Zen is a state of complete harmony between the mindful self and one's environment.

girlosophers

Marjorie Andres
Marjorie is 20 years old and from St Tropez, France. Marjorie's father is Spanish and her mother is French. She is currently studying marketing and international business and hopes to get her MBA.

Wendy Ash
Wendy is 20 years old and lives in Avalon, Australia. She works in sales and promotions. Wendy hopes to live overseas, preferably in Milan, in the future.

Isis Ashton-Mbye
Aged 23, Isis lives between Bali and Sydney. She is a singer and was recently signed to a major record company. Isis's mother is Australian and her father is from Gambia, Africa. Isis was five- months pregnant at the time she was photographed.

Mindy Dhanjal
Born in England, Mindy was brought up in Middlesex and London. Mindy's parents were born in India. After attending university, Mindy spent a year in France, before moving to Hong Kong. Mindy currently works for a Hong Kong television network as a children's television presenter.

Melina Dupont
Born in Lima, Peru, Melina is 24 years old and married with two children. Adopted by a French woman, she was brought to France at the age of 12 years. Melina lives with her family in St Tropez, France.

Ondine and Ella Gittoes
Ondine and Ella are sisters and live with their parents outside Sydney in Australia. Ondine, aged 4, is at kindergarten and Ella, aged 3, is in preschool.

Hannah Gunning
Hannah lives with her family south of Sydney, Australia. She is at school and wants to travel around the world when she is older 'to save all the animals'. She is eight years old.

Rebecca Hanlon
Rebecca is 24 and lives in Sydney, Australia, with her family. She works in retail sales and part-time as a production assistant, and would eventually like to work in media and entertainment.

Ita Jembrana
Ita's parents were born and lived in Jakarta, Indonesia, before moving to Bali, where Ita was born. Eighteen years old, Ita now lives in Denpasar, Bali, where she works as a dancer in traditional Balinese ceremonies.

Ashlie Keys
Ashlie is a college student majoring in travel. She lives in Collaroy, Australia, with her family, and hopes to travel both for work and pleasure in the future. Ashley is 19.

Natalie Lascelles
Born in France, Natalie moved with her family to England where she was raised. Natalie, now 31, is married with one child. She is studying naturopathy and kinesiology and currently lives in Sydney, Australia, with her husband and daughter.

Georgia Leary
Georgia lives in Palm Beach, Australia, and attends a nearby high school. Georgia is 16 years old and wants to work in the film industry when she finishes school.

Poppy McDonald
Poppy lives in Narrabeen, Australia, with her two-year-old daughter. Poppy is 23. Her mother is from Thailand and her father is Australian. Poppy was born in Sydney and has been working in the fashion industry.

Natalie Morris
Twenty-five years old, Natalie lives in Oxford Falls, Australia. She currently works as a hair stylist and is studying alternative healing therapies. Natalie is planning to travel after finishing her studies.

Indigo Ocean
Indigo is 32 and was born in Jamaica, New York. She moved to San Francisco some years ago and then to Bali, Indonesia, where she now lives and works as a spiritual dance teacher.

Ali Pickett
Ali lives in Avalon, Australia, with her family. She is 15 years old and is an active member of the Nepean Rowing Club. Ali is hoping to study costume design when she has finished high school.

Natalie Tester
Natalie lives in Narrabeen, Australia. Twenty-two years old, she works in retail sales and is currently saving to travel. Natalie loves cars and motorbikes and is 'just sort of cruising through life'.

Carla Tory
Carla is 18 and lives in Wollongong, Australia. Carla's mother is Indian and her father is Australian. A true beach girl, Carla works as a retail assistant for a major surf retail chain.

Favorite books

One of the most powerful steps on the road to self-definition and awareness is reading. Listening to music is another. Building a personal library and music collection is a bit like keeping a diary – you are collecting a history of your own journey, and each new addition can be viewed as another part of your personal tapestry. I rarely remember the specifics of activities or places nearly as well as I remember hearing a certain album or discovering the exact book I needed to read at a particular point in my life.

Here are a few of my favorite books. Some have been faithful and solid companions for me on countless occasions. Some are recent inclusions. I have always been delighted to be recommended a book by a friend and, accordingly, I recommend these to you now.

For the journey
Carlos Castaneda, *Journey to Ixtlan: The Lessons of Don Juan*, Penguin Books, London, 1973.
Robyn Davidson, *Tracks*, Picador, London, 1998.
Peter Matthiessen, *The Snow Leopard*, HarperCollins, London, 1979.
Brigitte Muir, *The Wind in My Hair*, Penguin Books, Ringwood, 1998.
M. Scott Peck, *The Road Less Travelled*, Simon & Schuster, New York, 1978.
Robert Pirsig, *Zen and the Art of Motorcycle Maintenance*, William Morrow & Co., New York, 1979.

For the self
Shakti Gawain, *Creative Visualization*, Bantam Books, New York, 1982.
Shakti Gawain, *Living in the Light*, Bantam Books, New York, 1993.
Jon Kabat-Zinn, *Wherever You Go, There You Are: Mindfulness Meditation in Everyday Life*, Hyperion, New York, 1994.
Robin Norwood, *Why Me Why This Why Now*, Arrow Books, London, 1994.
Stuart Wilde, *Infinite Self*, Hay House, Carlsbad, 1997.

For the body
Andrew Bell, *Creative Health*, Benton Ross Publishers, Auckland, 1989.
Louise L. Hay, *Heal Your Body*, Specialist Publications, Sydney, 1989.
Caroline Myss, *Anatomy of the Spirit*, Bantam Books, New York, 1998.

For the spirit
Deepak Chopra, *The Seven Spiritual Laws of Success*, Bantam Press, London, 1996.
Lama Surya Das, *Awakening to the Sacred*, Bantam Books, Sydney, 1999.
Khalil Gibran, *The Prophet*, Penguin Books, London, 1992.
Juan Mascaro (trans.), *The Bhagavad Gita*, Penguin Books, London, 1962.
Sogyal Rinpoche, *The Tibetan Book of Living and Dying*, HarperCollins, San Francisco, 1992.
Marianne Williamson, *A Return To Love*, HarperCollins, London, 1992.

For the girl-woman
Jessica Adams, *The New Astrology for Women*, HarperCollins, Sydney, 1998.
Mary Pipher PhD, *Reviving Ophelia*, Doubleday, Sydney, 1994.
Joan Smith, *Different for Girls*, Random House, London, 1998.
Marianne Williamson, *A Woman's Worth*, Random House, New York, 1993.
Naomi Wolf, *The Beauty Myth*, Vintage Books, London, 1991.

For the corporate girlosopher
Charles Handy, *The Hungry Spirit: Beyond Capitalism – A Quest for Purpose in the Modern World*, Arrow Books, London, 1998.
Anita Roddick, *Body & Soul*, Ebury Press, Great Britain, 1991.
Harriet Rubin, *The Princessa: Machiavelli for Women*, Bloomsbury, London 1998.

believe nothing, no matter where you read it or who has said it, not even if I have said it, unless it agrees with your own reason and your own common sense

buddha

So many thankyous

To the **Universe, Supreme Being, Spirit, God, Jah, Buddha:** thank you for my beautiful journey. I continue to be humbled. Special thanks to my **family**, especially my parents, **Sandra and Michael Paul**: there is so much to thank you for – everything in my wonderful, joyful and crazy life can be traced to you in some way and I am so grateful. It is a privilege to be your granddaughter, daughter, sister, niece and cousin. Hugest Love always.

To **Cathy Derksema**, my long-time creative collaborator, fantastic friend, ex-roommate, co-traveler and Cherokee Cherub. Thanks for the beautiful illustrations, for propping me up, inspiring me always and critiquing me honestly. We've only just begun – stoked!

To **Chris Jones**, for taking the breathtakingly beautiful pictures, for believing in the project from the beginning and for your razor-sharp vision in the studio and on location – love your work! Thanks, too, for helping me manage the post-production task so professionally and smoothly.

To **Andy, Lissa and Cayenne Barnum**, **Barnum Group Design**, for the stunning book and logo design, for the friendship and for the major support at every turn. Thanks to Special Cay for all the presents. XX

To **Jude McGee**, you were a gift from the Universe and I am indebted to you! Your good taste in editing and your unerring sense of what I wanted to create was the key to it all. Many thanks.

To **Sophie Cunningham, Simone Ford, Lou Playfair, Karen Williams, Angela Jonasson** and the fantastic team at **Allen & Unwin**, for understanding my vision and for making it happen in the best spirit, for being girlosophers off the bat . . . and for believing in me. Thank you very much.

To **Stuart Murray** and the production team at **Campbell Murray Creating**: many thanks.

To **John Martin**, thanks bucketloads for the positive energy exchange that I'd been hoping to find. You are hip wisdom and classic ab-fabulousness combined!

To **Julie Robb**, for the great advice, for structuring the deals so thoughtfully and for being one of the sanest people I know! I felt really comfortable knowing you were on board.

To **Andrew Mackenzie** and all at highlandertech.com.au – **Paul, Tom, Rob, Dana**: thanks heaps for making the coolest website for girlosophy.com. You really came through for me.

To **Jaime Marina**, for your contribution and for helping the bigger picture to become a reality.

To **Eddie and Jane Coffey** of **Peribo Fine Books**: thanks for your advice, support and referrals.

To **David Johnson**, for 'keeping me legit', for being a great sounding board for my peripatetic lifestyle between Sydney–NYC over the years, for helping the numbers to add up and for always remaining unfazed in the face of my newest adventure. Thanks for your positivity.

To **Tom Middleton**, for your brilliant musical taste (again) on the beautiful *girlosophy* CD. Many thanks. Who could have guessed where catfish, shampoo and the Seattle Bumbershoot Festival could lead us!

To **Bob McKendry** of Vision Graphics, for the meticulous post-production work; **Paul Nevin,** thank you for the great scanning job; and to **Julie Green** of **Exhibit A** for the beautiful black and white prints.

To **Skye and Hannah Gunning**: Flossie darling, for the longest-standing close relationship (24 years and still counting!) outside of my family that I'll probably ever have – you were there for the journey. Thanks always for your friendship, love and for understanding every aspect of the project and for calling at just the right time to say just the right things. To Hannah: it's way deep!!

To **Natalie Morris**, for your great work on location in Bali and for your positivity and spirit. You were a huge asset to the team. Thanks, too, for your friendship and for your dedication.

To the gorgeous and inspiring girls who appear in the pictures – **Hannah, Melina, Mindy, Indigo, Ita, Natalie L., Olivia, Natalie M., Natalie T., Wendy, Ali, Isis, Ondine, Ella, Carla, Poppy, Ashlie, Georgia, Marjorie, Rebecca**: XXX to each of you, a message with love. Thanks for your willingness and enthusiasm – it will always be remembered. Stay as natural and real as you were in these pictures throughout your lives, for you each exemplify inner and outer beauty and you are all very special – never forget it!

To **Paul Rafferty** and **Horse**, for being our minders on location.

A special thanks to the ever-gorgeous **Natalie Lascelles**, for being such a champion supporter and early girlosopher as well as being a great, willing and patient model.

To **Bianca Polinelli**, for always being able to make me laugh with the quickest (and best) comeback lines in

318

the business, for your friendship and for your assistance in many ways throughout the project. It's ON ! Ready?

To **Jessica Adams**, for being a fab friend, mentor, confidence giver, advisor and fellow Leo Grrrl and all-round astrobabe. You inspire me: onwards and upwards. Thanks for your many contributions.

To **Tim L'Estrange**: thanks for always being there and for being my favorite pocket Rottweiler!

To **Shelley Gare**, for so much – for sharing the vision and for your generosity of spirit in helping me to take it to another level, for caring, all the while juggling your own crazy schedule. You are truly inspiring – an amazon girlosopher and a great new friend for life.

To **Sandy Archer**, for taking a load off my mind with your expert handling of the admin side, for your advice and, of course, for the friendship too. Thanks always.

To **Catherine Martin**, Powerpoint Babe and girlosophy supporter. Thank you.

To **Bettina Andretic**, for supplying wardrobe and props as well as enthusiasm, support and friendship.

To **Kenny Ross**: you helped me to start the ball rolling back in NYC, late '96. Namaste. OM.

For angel-in-waiting **Marian Simms**: you are pure radiance and light. Many thanks for enlightening me, for seeing the beauty. It's precious. Thanks too for the great editing assistance.

To **Carole Muller**, for being such a great friend to me and also the whole family, for always welcoming me at Tirta Ayu, which gave me the strength to keep going, and for your excellent company.

To **Susan Katzen** and **Rod Dennington**: thanks for cooking for me all the times when I couldn't see straight after editing pictures all day! Love and Big Ups.

To **Yasmin Boland**, the most gorgeous alien of all (apart from Carole King): thanks for just being there and for contributing to the site, and here's to more fun spooky stuff in the future.

To **Mel Faragher**: Melly, you are so special, no matter where I am in the world, you always call me on the ESP line – amazing! Thanks for your input to the project – here's to many more years of long chats and hilarious stories, and I never minded when you got the time zone wrong – honestly! :)

To **Tricia and Justin Sgalia**: deepest gratitude for your friendship and for having me to stay in your lovely home in Long Beach in the summer of '98, which gave the manuscript a major boost. How do I love LA? :)

To **Marjorie Andres**: merci mille fois, cherie, tu es la plus belle fille et je t'aime beaucoup.

To **Rebecca Hanlon**, a real angel! Thanks for your assistance both on and off location.

To **Roxy Holder** and **Little Johnny**, for being such fantastic troopers and pitching in. Many thanks.

To **Ingvar Kenne**: Sweden and Hasselblad's finest export! Thanks for hooking me up and for all your support.

To **Treen**: you are a true individual. Thanks for your creative effort at the eleventh hour.

To **Jacqui Lane**, for doing the numbers with me and for the steely appraisal! Thank you.

To **Derek Hynd**: thanks for your perception regarding the project, marathon chats, surfing tips and for 'getting it'.

To **Suzanne and Piers Akerman**: thank you for listening and for your referrals to some great people.

To **Marty Dougherty**: your enthusiasm for the project was a major breakthrough for me and gave me the encouragement I needed as well as the confidence to persevere. Thank you.

To **Susan Duncan**, for your spot-on advice. Thank you and hugs to The Littles.

To **Peta Wilson**, for being so fearless and for teaching me a thing or two: thanks babe!

To **Gil Appleton**, for the referrals and advice. Thank you so much.

To **Tulli**, for keeping the office alive for me!

To **Earthly Goods** (Kangaroo Valley, Australia), **Tribes of the Earth** (Avalon, Australia), **BowWow** (Palm Beach, Australia), **Jiva** (Paddington, Australia), **Avalon Petworld** (Avalon, Australia), **Sacred River Retreat** boutique (West Bali, Indonesia): many thanks for the wonderful clothes, accessories, props and bunnies.

To **Sacred River Retreat, West Bali** – **Shankari, Dewa, Cainan, Omar, Raina, Karina, Marcus**: thanks to everyone for helping with shoot requirements above and beyond the call of duty.

To **Esky**: not a day goes by when I don't think of you. I miss you.

To **Bob Marley**, for the immeasurable creative inspiration you have given me throughout my life.

To **New York**: you gave me so many wonderful years. You make me, you break me and then – you make me again. You are extreme! You totally rule.

To **Bali** and **Jamaica**, my favorite resting places: you soothe my soul when I need it most.

To **Sydney**: you have my heart!